Family History in the Genes

For baby Alex and his mother

Family History in the Genes

Trace your DNA and
grow your family tree

Chris Pomery

the national archives

First published in 2007 by
The National Archives
Kew, Richmond
Surrey, TW9 4DU, UK

www.nationalarchives.gov.uk

The National Archives brings together the Public Record Office,
Historical Manuscripts Commission, Office of Public Sector
Information and Her Majesty's Stationery Office.

A catalogue card for this book is available from the British Library.

ISBN 978 1 905615 12 4

Typeset by Carolyn Griffiths, Cambridge, UK
Cover designed by Briony Hartley / Goldust Design
Printed by MPG Books, Bodmin, Cornwall, UK

Contents

Acknowledgements

In writing this book I've relied a lot upon the insights of others, and I specifically want to thank Patrick Guinness for his email correspondence over the years, notes on the Irish clans' study and his warm hospitality in Kildare; Susan Meates, convenor of the DNA Advisory Panel within the Guild of One-Name Studies; and Ann Turner, the always helpful former moderator of the Genealogy-DNA mailing list on Rootsweb. I also acknowledge a significant debt to the work of Stephen Oppenheimer, Spencer Wells, Dan Bradley and Brian McEvoy. Many DNA study organizers have helped me clarify my views during the past half decade including four members of the Guild of One-Name Studies: Orin Wells, Alan Savin, Susan Meates and Michael Dalton. Needless to say, the opinions in this book, and any errors, are entirely my own.

The publishing team at the National Archives, specifically Sheila Knight, my patient editor, and

Catherine Bradley, head of the publishing department, have done a great job to shepherd both me and the book to the point where the latter sits bound upon the shelves.

Lastly, my own thanks go to the nearly 1,400 Pomeroy family researchers across the globe who have helped me to build up the Pomeroy DNA project over seven years into one of the most comprehensive and developed of its kind, and to the board of the Pomeroy Family Association for part-funding it.

Picture sources

Front cover: A family on the beach, 1946 (Mirrorpix)

Back cover: A family on holiday in the Norfolk Broads, 1957 (John Drysdale/Keystone Features/Getty Images)

All other images can be seen at the National Archives.

p. 6 Children's Overseas Reception Board children travelling to New Zealand by boat, 1940–41 (DO 131/15)

p. 28 J. Noobner [sic], sculptor, in his London studio, 1883 (COPY 1/365)

p. 48 Golden wedding group of William and Mary Ann Mackereth, 1902 (COPY 1/456)

p. 74 Boys at Milton Board School, 1900 (COPY 1/160)

p. 118 Mother and daughter from Pears advertising poster, 1907 (COPY 1/514)

p. 132 Botswana (Bechuanaland) in Africa, 1960s (INF 10/61)

p. 160 Two celebratory family groups: the Mannings and the Passmores, 1901 (COPY 1/452)

p. 194 Local Jubilee treat group, Aldershot, 1887 (COPY 1/381)

p. 214 The Reverend Somers-Cocks and family, 1901 (COPY 1/453)

p. 220 Five generations of the Fleckney family, 1905 (COPY 1/481)

p. 230 Street view of St Kilda, from Scotland's Outer Hebrides, 1886 (COPY 1/377)

p. 236 Mr and Mrs Fowler return from church to the vicarage, Polesworth, 1906 (COPY 1/497)

Introduction: Everyone's heard about DNA

DNA testing is now part of our everyday lives. It is so commonplace that the principles behind the forensic criminal investigation procedures popularized in television series like *CSI Miami* and *Silent Witness* are barely explained as each episode airs. But this kind of investigation is just one of the many ways in which DNA testing is currently being used by scientists and researchers – and increasingly by family historians.

A forensic genetic test, for example, sets out to identify the unique human being that matches the DNA samples under analysis. It wants to find that one person from among the six billion of us on the planet, and to exclude everyone else. This close-up type of DNA search has been commercialized in DNA paternity tests and similar tests that measure very close relationships.

If forensic testing is like looking down a

microscope for a unique person, other kinds of DNA test are like looking through binoculars at the whole panorama of humanity. Several recent television series have used DNA testing to help people discover their connections with their most distant origins. In *Motherland* black Londoners were taken back to their ancestral homeland in Africa, while in *Blood of the Vikings* and *Face of Britain* people living today in the north of England were revealed to have a Norse or Viking heritage. This kind of DNA test isn't interested in uniqueness; it is looking for ways to link you with large groups of people who share at least one aspect of a common past.

This kind of wide-angle DNA analysis is possible because over the past 20 years or so scientists have mapped the pattern of changes that took place in mankind's DNA over the past 150,000 years with the physical migrations our ancestors made across the planet. By tracking minute changes in our DNA, researchers have confirmed that our most distant ancestors originated in Africa. In recent years their descendants' migrations have been mapped in increasing detail, and the genetic labels attached to these long-term population movements are gradually being brought closer to the present day, for example accounting for more modern movements such as the spread of the Vikings from their strongholds in Scandinavia to places like France and Britain.

Scientists are able to use genetic testing in such different ways because the tests they use measure different parts of our DNA. The tests on offer to family historians combine elements of both types of analysis, using the very slow long-term changes in our genetic make-up tracked by the migration scientists as well as the very quick short-term changes that the forensic scientists use to define the uniqueness of their samples.

The idea that DNA testing could be a useful tool for family historians is only as old as the new millennium. Back in April 2000 the BBC announced the results of Professor Bryan Sykes' ground-breaking Sykes DNA study. His conclusion was that all of the thousands of men in modern Britain bearing his surname essentially stem from a single, original Mr Sykes. A noted local-history expert even came up with the probable identity of this man in thirteenth-century Yorkshire.

Over the past eight years thousands of surname-oriented DNA projects, including my own Pomeroy project, have been set up.

Today, family history bulletin boards all over the web carry regular information about the progress of their DNA projects. More than a dozen genetics companies now offer DNA tests targeted at family historians, and more labs are gearing up to do so.

The scope of the DNA tests on offer has expanded too: there are now three types available. Surname-based DNA projects – the most common kind – use a specific test that targets the Y-chromosome. As this chromosome is found only in men, the transmission of this particular genetic data from father to son from generation to generation exactly mimics the handing down of surnames. A second type of DNA test allows researchers to track the female line of inheritance by measuring genetic data passed down from mother to daughter. And yet a third type of DNA test offers a general geographic picture of your overall genetic origins.

One thing to remember is that the result you receive from any DNA test will always need to be interpreted within an historical context, whether you have researched your family tree or not. While this book uses the British Isles as its geographical backdrop, the principles outlined will help you to understand your results within a

European context or when tracing an immigrant's family tree outside Europe.

I've tried to structure the book to make it an easy journey for someone who knows nothing whatsoever about DNA and genetics. Chapters 1–3 introduce the subject and the range of tests on offer. Chapters 4–6 look in detail at the three types of DNA test available to genealogists today. Chapter 7 gives some extended examples of successful projects, principally Y-chromosome surname projects, to show the standard that the most advanced projects are now reaching. Chapter 8 gives some basic advice on how to run your own DNA project, and Chapter 9 outlines some thoughts on how the environment may change in the years ahead. At the end there's a list of website addresses referred to in the book, a reading list of reference books, and a glossary of terms you will encounter as you read through the chapters.

When you hold the results of your DNA test in your hands, you are literally looking at yourself in a new light. I hope you'll find that this book helps you understand what you can learn from those results and what the different types of DNA test can teach you about your ancestry and family history.

Chapter 1

The brave new world of genetic genealogy

- Three timeframes
- The power of DNA testing
- When is a test useful?
- What approach should I take?
- Last thought

If you've started to research your family history, or are keen to find out who you are and where your ancestors came from, then you're reading the right book at the right time. Reconstructing your family tree is already easier to do today than at any point in the past, thanks to the growing amount of basic genealogical data available on the internet. And now new tools like DNA testing have the power to dramatically improve the quality of your research.

This is all very positive. But right from the outset one fact needs to be stated clearly: while a DNA test is a tool that you can use to help you build and verify your family tree, it is your tree itself, and the stories of the people in it, that make up your personal family history – not your DNA result.

Genetic testing, helpful though its results can be, shouldn't be considered a quick fix. No DNA result can replace the careful documentary research that is needed to recreate your family tree and to describe the lives of its members. But it certainly can be seen as a useful tool that has the potential to save you a great deal of time and money as you research, and to help you focus your attention in the right areas. Many researchers have found that their DNA results turn out to be simply invaluable.

Three timeframes

As you read through this book you'll notice that the knowledge that DNA results can supply falls into three historical timeframes, each offering different insights into your genetic and historical origins. You need to bear this in mind when you decide which DNA test is the right one for you.

- The first and most important timeframe lies in the modern era, from the present day back to the end of the medieval period around 1500 AD. This 500-year span is the era of documented records when surnames in England were passed down regularly from father to child. Within this timeframe you can reconstitute a forgotten family tree through diligent research on the web and in the archives, using DNA testing as a tool to guide and verify your research.

- The second timeframe lies a bit further back in history, in the period before surnames were well established, back to the times of the great classical writers who recorded at first hand what for us are the key events of ancient history. This fifteen-century long period runs from the middle of the last millennium back as far as the Roman occupation of Britain. Within this timeframe, your DNA test results might indicate whether your ancestors were participants in a well-known historical transition. For example, they might suggest a connection with the expansion of the Vikings from Scandinavia along the western Atlantic seaboard, or the westwards spread of the followers of Genghis Khan across Europe from their homelands in the Mongolian steppes.

- The third timeframe lies further back still, in a period that we understand today mainly through the archaeological record. This stretches from the first century AD back another ten thousand years or more to the end of the last Ice Age. Our understanding of this era is dominated by the absence of documentation. The insight your DNA results create relevant to this timeframe is therefore both new and unique.

The DNA tests available today can retrieve the faintest of echoes, stretching back tens of thousands of years, to the origin of two of your many thousands of ancestors. If you're of British origin the result should, for example, indicate roughly when those ancestors first arrived in Europe. It may hint at where in Europe they took refuge during the extreme cold of the last Ice Age, and it will almost certainly indicate how they fit into the story of the re-peopling of Britain after the glaciers retreated north and uncovered the land again some 12,000 years ago. Throughout this book I'll refer to this kind of knowledge as illustrating your 'deep ancestry', by which I mean any historical insight that is not of direct genealogical use.

In most of the pages in this book, however, I'll be focussing on the first of these three timeframes: the modern era from 1500 AD to the present day. That's not just because I want to bring out the importance of genes in the present-day practice of genealogy, but because this is the timeframe in which DNA testing can work as an effective research tool as you actively build up your family history.

It is a tool that can, in most contexts, be used precisely and confidently. Read carefully, your DNA result can tell you whether you share the same genetic heritage as someone else with your surname; in other words, whether the two of you belong in the same family tree and share the same direct paternal ancestor within the last 500–700 years. That, in a nutshell, is the power of a genealogical DNA test: in a moment, your DNA result can validate the documentary research that went into the reconstruction of your family tree, or it can suggest that you need to look at it again.

The power of DNA testing

In this book I'm going to describe the range of commercial DNA tests on offer at the time of writing and explain what you can expect to learn from each of them. I'll try to de-mystify the process for you, clarify the most common misunderstandings, and reduce the fear factor associated with the word 'DNA'. Along the way I'll relate some exciting examples of how family historians are using their DNA results to inform their family tree research, and give you a taste of promising new developments.

But let's start with a story which, for me, encapsulates the power and the beauty of DNA testing for family history researchers. As I said earlier, DNA testing is a tool: what it reveals becomes the heart of your personal story: your family's history.

About five years ago I received an email out of the blue from a Charles Pomeroy in the USA. Chuck, as he introduced himself, was an ex-Air Force officer, now retired. When stationed in Germany he'd taken time out several times to visit Ireland in search of his family's roots. Chuck had traced his Pomeroy family tree back to the 1750s, to an ancestor who arrived in Virginia, apparently from Ireland. As far as he could find out, that ancestor came from somewhere in the area around County Cork in the south of that country. For nearly 30 years Chuck had searched for a document that might link his own immigrant ancestor with any of the very few Pomeroy families in Ireland at the time, but he'd found nothing. As a last resort, he asked, could a DNA test possibly help him?

It often happens that, for various reasons, there is no DNA test currently available that can solve the specific query posed by your family tree. But in this instance I was able to assure Chuck that, yes, a standard Y-chromosome DNA test might well knock down this particularly 'brick wall' for him. This was so because substantial DNA research had already been carried out on holders of the Pomeroy surname. Within our group of surname researchers we'd been lucky enough to obtain DNA results from at least one member of most of our largest family trees. This matrix of results had grouped many of these men into a couple of 'genetic families'. In other words, based upon their DNA results, I could be reasonably sure that every member of each of these genetic families shared the same distant male Pomeroy ancestor; future research, we hope, will one day document that man's identity. Usefully for Chuck, two of these men, who share the same DNA result, also believed that their families traced their origins back to County Cork, coincidentally to the mid 1700s. Would Chuck's DNA result also turn out to be the same, revealing a direct relationship?

When Chuck's DNA result came back it clearly matched that of the two men of Irish origin. Chuck was delighted, for as clearly as could be asked the DNA test had revealed that the three of them belong within the same family tree. And as a bonus, the results for their wider genetic family hint that they may also be part of a much older and larger tree originating in the English region of the West Country, the historic heartland of the Pomeroy surname.

When is a test useful?

Chuck's experience is not uncommon, and it illustrates three of the most important characteristics of genealogical DNA matching that it is vital to keep in mind as you turn the pages of this book.

- The first point is that the genealogical value of your DNA test result is only created when you compare it with the results of other people's tests. Your result will, of course, be very different to most people's, similar to many people's but the same as only very few people's. It is up to you to decide who among this pool of potential matches is relevant to your family history research. In practice, this generally means people with your surname.

- The second point is that only two of your many lines of ancestry can be tested using the currently available tests: your direct paternal line and your direct maternal line. Whenever DNA testing firms – or this book – talk of 'finding your ancestry' they almost always mean your genetic ancestry as defined through one or both of these two lines. There is no test at present that you can take that can reveal precise details about any of your other lines, for example your grandmother's brother's line or your maternal grandfather's sister's. This may seem hugely restrictive because it excludes the majority of all of the branches in your family tree; indeed for many people it will mean that DNA testing is not the right tool for solving their particular research problem.

- The third point is that, of the two lines of ancestry that can be tested, the line of most common genealogical interest, the direct paternal line, can only be investigated by the results of a DNA test taken by men. As I'll explain later, that is a feature of the DNA test itself, not a social or gender restriction of any kind imposed by the labs running the tests.

Looking at these three points side by side they may seem at first glance to be hugely limiting. In practice the situation is not so bad, as most people, when they start to explore their family history, begin with their own surname, and for this line DNA testing is an option. The genealogical DNA test that is used to track the paternal line of descent from father to son, the line which is mirrored by the passing on of a surname, is known as a Y-chromosome test. The Y-test, as it is sometimes called, samples the DNA of the Y-chromosome. As the Y-chromosome is present only in men, it follows that only men can take this test.

Genetics companies are anxious – for sound commercial reasons – to develop a DNA test that will look at the X-chromosome, of which women have two copies and men just one, as well as DNA tests covering any of the other 22 pairs of chromosomes that we each have. Progress is being made in this area, but it will still be some time before simple DNA tests go on sale that can track ancestral relationships that cross back and forth between the male and female lines.

The counterpart to the paternal line Y-chromosome test is a simple DNA test that reveals the origin of the direct maternal line. Interestingly, this test was actually discovered before the Y-test. Two decades ago, when the scientists trying to recreate the spread of humanity across the planet started their work, they had already identified a bit of genetic material, found in both men and women, that was able to record long-term changes in humanity's DNA. What they used was mito-

chondrial DNA (or mtDNA as it is often abbre-
viated). This kind of DNA is passed down from
mother to child; one advantage of using it is
that the scientists can run an mtDNA test on
either men or women to identify the history of
their maternal line.

The results from tens of thousands of
mtDNA tests gave the scientists only half the
picture of our global genetic heritage: how
women had spread around the planet. It was
not long before the search began for a DNA
test that would help chart the spread of men
too. Logically, the scientists looked first at the
Y-chromosome, which only men carry. Today,
you can go to any DNA testing lab website and
you'll see that the surname-based test on offer
is a Y-chromosome test, while their mitochondrial DNA test is marketed as an ancestry test,
or as a female-line test, to both men and
women.

One limiting feature of mtDNA, from the
point of view of family historians, is that it is
only passed on from one generation to the
next by a mother through her daughter. A son
inherits it, but does not pass it on to his children; they will take their mtDNA from their
mother. While many people try to research the
direct female line in their family tree, finding

living female-line descendants of all the female ancestors stretching back up that line can be very challenging indeed. Each one has to be identified through a separate piece of research, which can be very time-consuming. The advantage of the Y-chromosome test is that the other potential test candidates are clearly identifiable right from the start: they are everyone else with the same surname.

What approach should I take?

The result of my personal Y-chromosome DNA test is shared by thousands of other men across the planet. As a family historian, however, I can see no benefit to learn that Fred Smith in Iowa and Bill Jones in California have the same Y-chromosome 'DNA signature' as mine. Why is this so? The DNA results are telling us that we share a common male ancestor, that is true, but the difference in surname indicates that the ancestor in question probably existed at a time well before surnames were established. In other words, there never will be a way to document the linkage between us or to help create a narrative family history that includes both of us. There's not even any way to know accurately how long ago our shared ancestor lived. So while it may be interesting for me to collect a list of all of the people I share that bit of my DNA with, and at best I may feel warm towards them as 'kin' of some kind, I'll never ever know how we are linked together.

By the same token there is no real point in DNA testing my brother as well as myself. We have a well-documented relationship and we don't need a DNA test to prove it. I can assume that my Y-chromosome result will be identical to that of my brother, my father, my paternal uncle, and to any other close male-line male relation. These are all people to whom I know I am related; a DNA test result won't tell me more than I already know.

In practice, I'm only interested in those men who have the same Y-chromosome result as mine and with whom I have a chance to discover a shared family history: that means, men who share my surname, or a potential variant of it. Within this sub-group of all the men that share my Y-chromosome DNA result I can be reasonably sure that the reason we share the same DNA and the same surname is that we both have the same paternal ancestor who lived in the period since surnames became established. And it follows that if we share the same direct paternal ancestry we will also share the same paternal deep ancestry heritage. With my family historian's hat on, these are the only results of immediate value to me.

With the mitochondrial DNA result I face two options: I can actively try and research through the records available to find the many descendants of my mother's maternal ancestry in order to prove my maternal line, or I can simply hope that one day someone else will record the same result and do that research for me. Given the huge scale of this kind of family history research it's not surprising that few people undertake it and that few links revealed through mtDNA testing have been documented. And, of course, I will have the same mtDNA result as many other people through a direct maternal line ancestor we share as long ago as many thousands of years, but these are always going to be completely undocumentable connections.

We may want DNA testing to play a role in solving the documentary gaps and problems in other parts of our family trees, but there are sound reasons why this is going to be difficult to achieve. Targeting the direct paternal line and the direct maternal line is a start, but ten generations back my tree should contain as many as 1,024 individual direct ancestors.

What DNA test can you use to track those outside of the direct male and female lines?

Well, the simple answer is that there is no suitable test as yet. Any problem in your family tree in any line that switches at some point between the male and female line of descent cannot at present be DNA tested. While that may seem very disappointing indeed, given that most people's 'brick walls' concern a father's mother's uncle or some other similarly indirect relationship, an answer may present itself over time. That's because another researcher somewhere may be running a DNA surname project for the surname of that person, and the answer you seek may turn out to be visible in their results and their family tree reconstructions. But we are many years away from a universal DNA test that can unravel any question in our family tree.

Last thought

The lesson to take away from this chapter is that one must always think of the surname as the basic unit of DNA analysis. As a genealogist I don't need a DNA test to prove that my father and I have the same DNA; we assume this is so because we can document our relationship (and because we look alike). What I need is a test that will tell me which, out of all the other men that share my surname, are the ones with whom I also share a common paternal ancestor. Y-chromosome testing is a uniquely powerful tool to facilitate the reconstruction of family trees built around a common surname. It can often do that job extremely well, in a way that no other tool can, but like most tools it is not so well suited to other jobs. Mitochondrial DNA results can be used in a similar way, but because there are no common surnames involved this requires a great deal more effort to research, both to find someone relevant to test and to document your link with anyone you genetically match.

Now that we've set out a framework for thinking about DNA tests, in the next few chapters we'll look in more detail at the different types of test and how they are being used. But first, let's look at some of the simple scientific principles underpinning these types of genetic test. It will help to understand them before exploring the subject much further.

Myths about DNA testing

'DNA testing is only for advanced genealogists with years of research behind them.'

Many of the largest DNA projects are indeed run by experienced family historians, but the real utility of a DNA test is that it can save you years of fruitless endeavour by directing you in the right direction at a very early stage. Where once your quest started with the search for documents to fill the blank space at the top of your family tree, a DNA test can provide you with the names and email addresses of other researchers with whom you can be confident you share a recent ancestor. In many cases one of these will have already done a great deal of the relevant historical research, leaving you with the much easier task of connecting to an already established tree.

'DNA testing is painful. I hate giving blood and don't have time to do it anyway.'

Rest assured, the tests marketed to genealogists would be much less popular if they required you to give blood! The centrepiece of the test kit is a swab stick that's a bit like a cotton bud. All that's required is that you rub it around inside your mouth a few times, a process less time-consuming than cleaning your teeth and less risky than cutting your nails. In fact the tricky part of taking a DNA test is not the sampling process itself, but sorting through all the paperwork that gives the testing lab permission to process your sample.

'When you send off your sample you lose control over it. The testing company can do what it likes with your sample and your results.'

Er, no! Depositing your DNA sample with an accredited lab is a bit like putting your money in the bank. The institution holds it on trust, but you own it. As the donor, you also have the right to ask for your DNA to be destroyed after you've received your results. Companies and universities are bound by strict ethical rules governing their handling of DNA samples and results: if they break these, they risk the loss of public funding for their research projects. That's a very stout stick hanging over them.

'Suppose my health insurance company gets hold of my DNA data and finds a reason to increase my premiums?'

Given that your insurance company probably asked you to complete and sign a detailed health questionnaire, they surely have more than enough data to inform them of the 'risk' that you represent to them. You'll remember that they had to ask permission from you to view your medical records? Your DNA results are no less secure. They don't need your DNA, and even if they did they'd only need to follow you around for a few minutes in order to pick up a sample of it. Every day without worrying you shed millions of dead cells — each of which contains your DNA signature — everywhere you walk and every time you rest.

'DNA testing is the one-stop turbo-powered solution to your genealogical research.'

Would that it were so! It is true that the value of a DNA test result is growing all the time simply because the number of people with results to compare with is rapidly increasing. But the day is still a long way off when your DNA result will generate a family tree for you. What may happen, and sooner than we might imagine, is that the growth of online networks linking different family trees together might provide that answer. Even then your DNA result will be extremely useful for you to confirm the accuracy of that online matching process.

Chapter 2

How the DNA test works

- How safe is it?
- What are the medical implications?
- The test kit
- Interpreting your test results
  Your genetic material
  More about mutations
  The features of test markers
  What are you trying to prove?

If you've never contemplated taking a DNA test before you may well hesitate when someone suggests that you buy a test kit. There are reasons for doing so: it's a complicated business, built around hi-tech science, with huge implications for your personal privacy. Goodness, DNA testing is something criminals are made to do, isn't it?

There are many myths surrounding DNA testing, but most of them don't bear much scrutiny. The one caveat that you should bear in mind is that the result you get back from your test may not be the one that you are expecting. It may threaten to overturn all the stories you have inherited about your family and your ancestry, and it may even undo all the work that you've put into researching your family tree. If you think that kind of surprise might upset you then the best thing to do is not to take a DNA test. In my experience, however, many more people end up disappointed with their results not because a dark family secret has been brought to light but because the results are inconclusive. If you are the only person with your surname who has your Y-chromosome DNA result it can feel a little lonely: where have all those expected genetic matches gone to?

How safe is it?

One myth often repeated is that your DNA is not safe inside the lab that is testing it. Other people might get access to your DNA: who knows what they might do with it? In practice, there are multiple safeguards at each stage of the test process that are designed to protect your privacy. For example, the lab performing the test will probably only know your sample as a number; the company selling you the test will hold the additional detail of your identity. When you submit your DNA sample you will be asked to sign a consent form that allows the two firms to do certain things to process it; there are risks to them if they act in ways without your consent. Their agreement with you will, for example, likely bar them from passing your result to a third party or letting your DNA sample leave their lab. Some people in Britain also worry that their DNA is being sent to a lab in the United States, though the restrictions the labs work under there are as strong as they are in Europe.

You can take reassurance from the fact that there are many features about DNA testing that put a different perspective on these kinds of concerns. Perhaps the best reassurance is the sheer number of researchers who are willing to share their data. There are several data-bases of DNA results on the web that have been built up using data submitted voluntarily by people just like you and I. These databases are designed to let you, and everyone else, search for specific DNA results and to contact their owners. Clearly these people would not be advertising their results online if they were afraid they could be misused.

Another sign is its acceptance by the market leaders in the field of genealogy. Most recently, the largest genealogy company in the world, The Generations Network Inc, announced in 2007 that its Ancestry.com web-site will soon include DNA result data along-side the traditional family trees and bulletin boards. The sheer number of DNA tests now being undertaken – several hundreds of thousands in the past few years – indicates that an increasing number of people see no risk in publishing the results of their genealogical DNA tests to the world, but only benefits.

What are the medical implications?

It's reasonable to be concerned that a DNA test could reveal details of your medical history that you choose not to know or that you might wish to keep private. But with the exception of a single, extremely rare Y-chromosome test result found at just one marker out of dozens in regular use, after nearly 10 years of use we can still say that the results of a genealogical DNA test won't reveal anything about any medical condition that you have or are predisposed to have. The results cannot even directly reveal your race.

The thing to realize about the DNA tests used by family historians is that they look at only a very tiny part of the entire genetic spectrum of your genes. While the function of your DNA as a whole is to organize the replication of a new human being in all its complexity, not every part of it actually has an active role in that process. The genetic information measured in the tests that genealogists use has been selected precisely because that DNA has no direct function in the replication process. In fact, within the scientific community the DNA used in the Y-chromosome test is often referred to as 'junk DNA'.

So the results that you get back from a genealogical DNA test are designed to have only a very limited usefulness: to define a DNA signature for you that you can compare with those of other people.

The test kit

The process of taking a DNA test is simple and painless. The kit sent by the lab will usually contain a sterile cotton swab which you scrape across the inside of your mouth a few times before mailing it back to the lab in a sealed envelope. There are in fact several ways to collect a DNA sample reliably: one lab even asks you to chew some gum and mail that back. Every lab will ask you to provide more than one sample just in case the first becomes contaminated by accident by yourself or in the lab. It's important at this stage to read the instructions that come with the kit, which include advice such as not taking a hot drink immediately before providing your sample. You will also be asked to sign a consent form as described above.

Trapped in the cotton swab that you return to the lab are thousands of dead cheek cells. Inside the lab these cells are isolated and teased apart to reveal the simple coded message held within your DNA.

Interpreting your test results

The lab process generally takes three to six weeks to complete. The format of the results' package depends on the type of DNA test you took and the lab you chose to process it. In this chapter I'll use the Y-chromosome test results as my example simply because this test is the most commonly taken and, potentially, the most complex to understand.

A Y-chromosome test result itself is easy to read – the complications only start when you begin to compare your result with those of other people. The lab will present it to you in a simple numerical format, as shown below.

Sample 10-marker Y-chromosome result

Marker name

19	388	390	391	392	393	389i	389ii	425	426
Your result									
14	12	24	10	13	13	13	29	12	12

The table shows the names of specific places on the Y-chromosome (the marker names) where the lab has tested the chemical composition of your DNA. The result they found is expressed as a numerical value. Your overall Y-chromosome test result is, in effect, a string of numbers. You can think of this string of numbers as your personal Y-chromosome DNA signature.

To understand your test result you don't need to grapple with the science behind it. What you do need to understand are the few concepts explained in the rest of this chapter.

The fundamental principle underlying all DNA tests is that our DNA is handed down from one generation to the next according to fixed rules. When it comes to the Y-chromosome, the process of genetic copying allows for only minute variations between the DNA of a father and the copy of that DNA given to his son. When analyzing Y-chromosome results we therefore make the assumption that the DNA signature of a man taking the test is identical to that of his father, his father's father and so on, back through the generations along that direct paternal line.

Occasionally, though, some small changes do occur from one generation to the next: these are known as genetic mutations and they are the feature of DNA that allows us to see meaningful differences between individual DNA signatures. A genetic mutation is simply a glitch in the process of copying the DNA from parent to child. Scientists have a rough idea how often mutations occur from generation to generation, and the current thinking is that, over the 700-year timeframe which is the focus of a genealogical researcher, mutations are quite rare. Within the context of a surname analysis, when comparing a set of results of men with the same surname, we can say that those with the same or very similar Y-test result are likely to be related (and thus to be members of the same family tree) and those with markedly dissimilar results are not genetically related (and therefore not likely to be members of the same family tree).

Let's use the results in the table below to show how these principles work in practice. We'll start by comparing several Y-chromosome results with each other.

Sample 10-marker Y-chromosome results

19	388	390	391	392	393	389i	389ii	425	426
John SMITH									
14	12	24	10	13	13	13	29	12	12
Doug SMITH									
14	12	24	10	13	13	13	29	12	12
Fred SMITH									
14	11	24	10	13	13	13	29	12	12
Bill SMITH									
14	12	25	11	14	15	11	28	12	12
Alf TURNER									
14	12	24	10	13	13	13	29	12	12
Geoff TURNER									
14	12	25	11	14	15	11	28	12	12

Firstly, we can see that John Smith and Doug Smith have identical results: the numerical values are the same on all markers. Fred Smith's result is almost the same, except that on marker #388 he has the value 11 while John and Doug have 12. Bill Smith's result, however, is markedly different. His values are different from John Smith's on six of the ten markers. Turning to look at the two Turner results we can see that Alf Turner's result is the same as those of John and Doug Smith while Geoff Turner's result is the same as Bill Smith's and different from that of his name-sake Alf.

The process of interpreting these results is straightforward. John, Doug and Fred look to be related to each other because their DNA signatures are identical, or almost identical, and they share the same surname. Alf Turner's result is the same as that of both John and Doug Smith, but the fact that he has a differ-ent surname would lead us to suspect that the common paternal ancestor he shares with them pre-dates the period when surnames were adopted.

Bill Smith is not genetically related to the other three Smiths as his DNA signature is very different, so his Smith line most likely had a different paternal ancestor who adopted the Smith surname at another time and in another place. If, however, we know that Bill has been documented as a member of the same family tree as John, Doug and Fred, then we need to explain why his DNA signature is different

from theirs. If that is so then clearly somewhere along the line of his direct paternal
ancestry someone else's Y-chromosome DNA
has been substituted for the DNA signature
held by the shared ancestor of Bill, John, Doug
and Fred.

At this point one might leap to the conclusion that perhaps one of Bill's male Smith
ancestors was illegitimate (i.e. where the son
took the Smith surname from his mother
rather than his father), or that one of the wives
of his male Smith ancestors conceived a son
from someone other than her husband, but
there are a host of other ways in which surnames and DNA signatures can diverge, as
we'll see in a later chapter. A non-Smith relation might, for example, have adopted the
Smith surname in a legal move as part of an
inheritance arrangement.

It might be tempting to suggest that the donor
of the interloping DNA in Bill Smith's line was
provided by an ancestor of Geoff Turner because
their DNA results are identical, but this is not a
good hypothesis to make based upon the DNA
results alone: there will be many thousands of
other men with different surnames who share
this identical DNA signature. The linkage could
equally be with any one of them.

Your genetic material
With the basic principles of mutation and comparison now clear in our mind, this is a good moment to explain why the migration scientists, the geneticists who developed the first generation of genealogical DNA test, chose the Y-chromosome and mitochondrial DNA in the first place.

The DNA of each of us contains 23 pairs of chromosomes, one pair of which decides our gender. A child inherits the decisive chromosome – the options are labelled X and Y – from its father. If it inherits a Y-chromosome to make an XY pair it will always become a boy; if it gets an X-chromosome from its father to match the X-chromosome from its mother making an XX pair, it will be a girl.

The DNA data in the other 22 pairs of chromosomes is passed on from the father or the mother, and in the creation of each new child the original data from both parents undergoes a mixing process, known as recombination, to form each new chromosome in the egg or sperm that will join to create the child. The Y-chromosome, however, does not undergo recombination; it is passed down intact from father to son. This is true also of mitochondrial DNA, which confusingly is separate from the

23 chromosomal pairs. It also is passed from one generation to another without undergoing recombination. When the scientists were originally looking for a non-recombining bit of DNA to use to track migrations they first hit upon mitochondrial DNA; later, looking for a male gender equivalent, the non-recombining Y-chromosome was the obvious counterpart.

More about mutations

As we have seen, if the non-recombining mtDNA and Y-chromosome DNA was always passed down from one generation to the next without any change, everyone on the planet would have the same DNA signature when taking those two DNA tests. But they don't, and the differences between individuals are accounted for by mutations. There are lots of types of these, but the three most common are the accidental copying of a small segment of DNA data twice, the omission of a small segment of data during the copying process, or the transference of a segment from one place in the chromosome to another. And it will come as no surprise to find out that the DNA measured at all the different markers mutate at different rates.

When scientists were trying to unravel the

migration history of humankind they were looking for DNA markers with a special characteristic: those that had mutated only once, in one human at one time and in one place, creating a new marker value that would then be held by every single one of that person's descendants and by no others. By sampling present-day populations around the world for these one-time-only mutations it became possible to see where that mutating individual's descendants had moved to. By working backwards the scientists could estimate the time when each mutation had occurred and the rough geographical area where that individual had lived when the mutation occurred. Today with several hundred of these one-time-only markers being used, the migration map of humankind is coming into ever clearer focus.

A different group of scientists, the forensic scientists currently so popular in television dramas, were looking for markers exhibiting the completely opposite behaviour. They needed markers that mutated so often that an individual's values for each of the markers was much closer to being randomly decided. The standard police DNA databases use 13 highly variable markers, a great enough number that the odds of two people having the same set of values for the entire string of 13 markers is several billions to one.

If one was designing a genealogical DNA test from scratch one would try to use markers that mutate from time to time – otherwise the results for most people would look very similar indeed – but do not mutate so often that people who are known to be related do not appear to be genetically linked. The markers would have to mutate sometimes, but not too often. It would be even better if some markers mutated slightly more often than others: this would allow us to grade the differences between the markers when comparing two DNA signatures.

The markers in the Y-chromosome tests offered to family historians, however, were not designed from scratch for genealogical purposes. Instead, starting with a handful of markers that were discovered a few decades ago, their number has grown over time as different labs have identified new ones. Certain markers are popular with the genetics labs because they can be measured simply and effectively, but if you compare the Y-chromosome tests offered by different labs you'll see that while they often use unique markers, there is a great deal of overlap. There's little likelihood now that the first set of markers – even those which have turned out to be not particularly useful – will ever be dropped from the standard genealogical Y-chromosome test, for the simple reason that tens of thousands of men have already received their DNA results including them. As I mentioned before, the only value of a DNA result is to compare it with other people's, so if a marker has been used for a long time already it is likely to continue to be used in future. The opposite is also true: there's no point in using unusual markers that no one else has had tested, because comparisons will not be possible, at least not for some time.

The features of test markers
The markers that the Y-chromosome genealogical DNA tests use are broadly similar to each other, but have some different features that we need to consider.

The first key difference between markers is their relative propensity to mutate. Some markers appear to mutate fairly often: these have been dubbed 'fast' markers. Others appear to mutate relatively infrequently and are consequently known as 'slow' markers. Precise numerical rates of mutation have not, as yet, been agreed, so categorizing the markers into these two groups is still a work in progress.

A second difference between markers is the ease with which the lab can obtain an accurate result during the testing process. Some of the markers used in commercial Y-tests are different in that the result is not expressed as a single number but is split into a pair of values, or sometimes even four values. The ability of the labs to pinpoint accurate results for these unusual markers can be less than reliable. It can be irritating if the two DNA signatures you are comparing look different because of a difference in the value recorded on one of these multiple markers: you can't be sure if the difference is a real one that exists in the DNA as a result of mutation or an apparent difference caused by a problem interpreting the result in the lab.

What are you trying to prove?

By now you might be wondering just how useful genealogical DNA tests really are! But don't worry; most comparisons will actually deliver a clear result one way or the other. The challenge comes when two results look a bit the same and at the same time a bit different. It can be hard to tell which they are: similar, or different?

Judging these cases is best decided by the context, for example if we are using the DNA results to test the hypothesis that two men share a direct paternal ancestor. In this case we are asking the results to deny that this hypothesis is true; simply by looking at the DNA data in this way it becomes easier to form an opinion. Remember, DNA testing is a tool and the main job that we are asking it to perform is to confirm our existing knowledge of our family tree.

With or without a hypothesis, the process of comparing test results is always the same. The differences between any two sets of results are counted, starting with the slowest-mutating markers and then the faster-mutating markers. In many cases it will be obvious just by looking at the differences within the slow-mutating markers that the two results do not indicate a recent shared male ancestor.

*

One of the important lessons a genealogist should take away from this chapter is that there may be fewer black-and-white answers than one might expect, even though DNA testing is a scientifically credible activity: there are a great many more variables and unknowns in play than one might have at first thought. The good news is that many of these unknowns are in the process of being defined as more DNA test results are published worldwide, so the interpretation process should get easier as time goes on.

This has already happened to some extent in recent years, during which the number of test markers in the standard DNA test has increased. Today the highest-resolution Y-chromosome tests offer as many as 67 markers, a medium-resolution test 37–43 markers and a low-resolution test around 25. Just a few years ago the standard test offered just 12 markers while the original academic paper using DNA as part of a surname analysis cited only 4 markers. That marks a big improvement in the overall quality of results, and allows us to be more confident in making comparisons between DNA signatures.

Chapter 3

Choosing a test and testing company

- The Y-chromosome test
  Uses of the test
- The mitochondrial test
- Genetic heritage tests
- The testing process
- How to select a testing company
  Online assistance
  Size of the firm's results database
  Test costs and savings
  Number of markers measured
  Sample storage

There are three types of DNA test that commercial companies are marketing to genealogists. As we have seen, the first is the Y-chromosome test aimed at men and used in thousands of surname reconstruction projects now under way around the world. The second is the mitochondrial DNA test which is aimed at both men and women; its results reveal the maternal line heritage of the person taking the test and can sometimes be used to answer a specific family history question. The third kind of test sets out to define a person's overall genetic heritage.

The Y-chromosome test

The DNA test that most genealogists will end up buying is the Y-chromosome test. Just to recap, the Y-chromosome test – sometimes described as a Y-line or Y-test – can only be taken by men. The DNA in the Y-chromosome is passed on from father to son. In this process, basically unchanged from generation to generation, it mimics the other feature that a father passes to his son: his surname. All the male members of a family that bear the same surname and who stem from the same single male ancestor at the top of their family tree should possess the same Y-chromosome DNA signature.

The message hidden in their DNA reveals that they share a genetic ancestor; the message implied by their shared surname is that that common ancestor lived since the wide-scale adoption of surnames. Put another way, there might be 50,000 men in Britain with the same Y-chromosome DNA result as mine, but the only ones of interest to me when I'm building my family tree is the tiny fraction of that number who share my surname.

Uses of the test
There are many ways in which the Y-chromosome test can be useful for family historians.

At its simplest it can reveal whether two men who share the same surname also share the same DNA signature, and hence belong in the same family tree. This process of comparison can, however, be scaled up from just two individuals to include dozens of men, families or family trees, or indeed every single man that shares the surname.

In practice, because it is greatly advantageous to compare your result with as many potential matches as possible, at the point when you sign up for your own Y-chromosome test it is important that you check with the company whether a DNA project has already been registered for your surname. By signing up for your test from inside a surname project you not only access the reduced prices offered to group members by the testing company but you can be certain that your results will be compared within the most potentially useful pool of results.

Some surname-based DNA projects are linked to documentary research projects dedicated to recreating the family trees of everyone carrying that surname. If you are very fortunate indeed your decision to take a DNA test may lead you directly to someone who has already researched your particular family tree in great detail.

As the number of results within a surname-based DNA project grows, what tends to happen is that they group together into clusters of identical or near-identical DNA signatures. So, for example, in a project that has tested a dozen or so men, four or five may find that they share a common DNA signature, as will two other pairs of men, while the remaining testees will each have a unique result, meaning that they have so far not found any DNA matches within their surname.

This process of grouping together those surname bearers with the same DNA signature is described as building genetic families. Each genetic family is really a short list of men with the same surname who, based upon the clues given by their DNA results, look as though they share the same male ancestor. Identifying genetic families is the basic activity of any surname-based DNA project, and though it sounds straightforward it can require you to balance a number of factors when weighing up a judgement on borderline cases. Here's how it can work in practice.

Let's say hypothetically that 20 males with my surname Pomery take a DNA test and seven of them are found to have an identical Y-chromosome result. We'll assume that at the time of the test none of the seven can document a link between the ancestor at the head of their own family tree and any of the other trees. What the DNA results have created is a broader genetic family encompassing all seven of these men, and their trees, into one yet-to-be documented family tree. Each of the men tested now has a new focus for his family history research: finding links with the trees of the other men. Their DNA results have offered them the clear hope that they will find links with six other men's trees as well as telling them which six trees among the total of 19 to focus on. Another part of that focus is the news that they don't need to look right now at finding links with the other 13 surname bearers who have different DNA results.

Some of the seven might already have suspected that they could be related, particularly if some of their ancestors lived in the same small geographical area in a remote part of the country. But it often happens that the trees grouped together by the DNA results into a genetic family seem to originate in places that are very far apart and where there is no obvious historical connection. It's these cases that show the immense value that DNA testing can bring to our generation of genealogists: evidence of linkages like this are unlikely to come from any other source. Compared to the costs of researching a family tree over many years, the price of a DNA test to uncover this quality of information starts to look very good value for money indeed.

In Chapter 4 we'll look in detail at how one analyzes groups of Y-chromosome results, and in Chapter 7 at the kind of results the most advanced projects have discovered.

The largest surname projects

Men tested in registered surname projects at Family Tree DNA* (totals include some variants)

Anderson	204	MacLaren	261
Baker	290	Martin	212
Bassett	216	May	168
Bates	167	Meates	259
Bolling	259	Moore	232
Brown	421	Morrison	181
Butler	152	Payne	150
Campbell	247	Phillips	158
Carpenter	157	Rice	201
Carter	215	Rose	403
Chandler	161	Spencer	170
Cook	174	Stewart	225
Cooper	194	Taylor	173
Crow	199	Thompson	188
Davis	274	Turner	256
Gordon	167	Walker	427
Greaves	320	Webb	164
Hamilton	229	West	152
Harris	234	White	151
Hill	260	Williams	437
Johnson	413	Wilson	239
Jones	182	Wright	200
Lewis	219		
MacGregor	280		
Mackenzie	156		

* In August 2007

The mitochondrial test

The second type of DNA test on offer is the mitochondrial DNA test. This is completely different from the Y-chromosome test in several ways. Firstly, both men and women have mitochondrial DNA, whereas only men have Y-chromosome DNA. Secondly, the pattern of mitochondrial DNA is passed down the generations from mother to daughter, whereas the Y-chromosome DNA is passed down from father to son. While mothers transmit their mitochondrial DNA to all of their children, boys as well as girls, the boys when they grow up do not pass it on to their children. Sisters share an identical mitochondrial DNA signature, the same as their mother and *her* sisters. The mitochondrial DNA test therefore tracks the female line of descent.

Because the difficulties of researching female lines are so much greater than when researching male lines, in practice the mtDNA test is used only to try to solve very specific genealogical queries. The mtDNA test doesn't have a generic application in the way that the Y-chromosome test results will always reveal data that is potentially useful to every other bearer of the same surname. We'll look in detail at the mitochondrial DNA test and its uses in Chapter 5.

Genetic heritage tests

The third kind of DNA test on offer can best be described as the 'genetic heritage' test. These tests come in a variety of shapes, sizes and flavours, depending on the company offering them and the marketing pitch used to attract potential clients. In Chapter 6 I describe the tests on offer in 2007 one by one so you can see what they have in common and how they vary, but let's have a quick look at the two broad types around today.

- The first type of test aims to describe your overall *genetic make-up*. It takes a wide-angle picture of your deep-ancestral DNA heritage, and unlike the other types of DNA test analyzes markers taken from across the entire set of your chromosomes, not just the Y-chromosome and mitochondrial DNA alone.

- The second type of test attempts to be much more specific. It tries to link you with a specific group of historical people such as a tribe. These *tribal identification* tests often use standard Y-chromosome and mitochondrial DNA results and then add a specialist interpretation to link particular DNA signatures as typical of specific tribes or to signal a particular geographical origin.

Heritage DNA tests are widely marketed nowadays but they are really of only marginal interest to family historians, whose overriding goal is to document their family tree as far back as they can. A genetic heritage test will only, in very rare cases, provide useful clues for a genealogist.

At this point I can see a hand waving frantically at the back of the class. Why is it, you might well ask, that the tribal identification tests, which are based upon results from the standard Y-chromosome test, produce results that a family historian can use to find his surname-related ancestors?

The main answer is that not all of these genetic heritage tests supply results that can usefully be compared with the results of other people. They may claim to tell you some interesting things about your personal genetic heritage, but the results as supplied do not always come in a format that is always comparable with standard Y-chromosome results obtained inside a surname DNA project. If it is important to you that they *are* in the same format, check carefully before you buy.

The second answer relates to the three timeframes mentioned in the first chapter. Quite simply, the results of a genetic heritage test relate to a different timeframe from the one that interests family historians. In some cases the standard genealogical Y-chromosome DNA test has indeed provided useful results on a slightly longer timeframe than that associated with the rise and spread of surnames. Good examples are several studies of Irish and Scottish clans with results tending to confirm their oral histories, which stretch into the first millennium of British history. Genetic heritage tests, however, attempt to reach back even further in time, for example to identify Viking raiders and settlers in Britain around 1,200 years ago or the Pictish inhabitants of Scotland 2,000 years ago. Clearly a family historian can see a use for a DNA test that links different individuals who share a common surname, and different surnames within a single clan, or even different clans. But there is no practical benefit if I know, for example, that my DNA signature, within the context of an attempted tribal identification, is akin to that held by two-thirds of the British population. It's simply not going to advance my family history at all.

Finally, there's still a deal of scepticism about the integrity of the genetic heritage tests. Even though many of the companies offering these tests have been set up by respected academics, others in the academic community believe that the tests promise more than they can deliver. Though the tests may be built upon knowledge gained from the earliest population and migration studies, the conclusions they reach are, at best, still open to revision. Indeed, one of Britain's leading genetics experts, Mark Thomas at University College in London, recently likened this kind of test to 'genetic astrology' – though perhaps we can be charitable and say that future tests may yet become more specific and useful.

The testing process

Regardless of the type of DNA test you take and your choice of testing company, the process of taking the test is broadly similar in almost every case.

- *Stage one* requires you to decide why you are taking a test and what you want to find out by doing so. You need to have this clear in your mind in order to select the type of test that can potentially answer your research question.

- *Stage two* is to identify the test companies offering your chosen type of test. There are several websites that discuss the merits of the different companies, and I've included details in the chapters that follow.

- *Stage three* is to order your test kit. All the testing companies handle the vast majority of their orders over the internet, but they will also advertise a phone number that you can call if you want to order a test kit in person. Some companies will bill your credit card when they dispatch the test kit, so the onus will be on you to return it, while others will wait to bill you until they have received your DNA sample, which gives you the chance to change your mind after you've ordered the kit.

- *Stage four* is for you to provide your DNA sample using the kit posted to you by the testing company. This I briefly described in Chapter 2, but for the sake of completeness, here's a recap. The test process is really very simple. Inside the kit will be a sampling device, which is usually a cotton-tipped swab. You put this in your mouth and move it around gently for a few seconds against the inside of your cheek. As it passes over your skin the swab picks up the dead cells that lie on the surface, each one of which contains the genetic data the lab needs to read your DNA result.

The labs will provide you with more than one swab stick and will ask you to take two or more samples at different times. The only reason they do this is to ensure that at least one sample contains enough DNA for the lab to run a successful test. It can also happen that a sample becomes contaminated, for example if you put it down on a table top before placing it in the return package provided, or if you drink a hot cup of tea before using the swab (this removes most of the dead cells the swab is designed to pick up). Either way, a second or subsequent swab is simply a back-up in case the first swab cannot be processed by the lab as expected. With your samples done, you simply post the kit back to the testing lab.

- *Stage five* is when you receive the results back from the test lab. In most cases this will be within 3–5 weeks of your samples

being received. The format they are presented in will vary, but will usually comprise
a report that gives you the actual results
(that is, the numerical values for each
marker tested). The ability of your lab to provide you with meaningful information is
largely dependent on the number of test
results already held in its internal database
which it can use for comparison. That said,
the lab's report is really only a starting point
for you in the process of building an understanding of the significance of your personal
DNA result. When you are buying a DNA
test you are not paying the lab to interpret
the result for you in detail, even within its
own database, only to identify the result so
that you can make comparisons yourself.

- *Stage six* covers the steps you take to make
  those comparisons and to increase your
  understanding of what your DNA result
  means. I cannot stress too often that the
  real value of a DNA test lies in the comparisons you are able to make with other
  people's results. If you are taking part in a
  surname Y-chromosome project, your first
  comparison will be with the results of the
  other members of this group. But even if

you do not belong to a surname-based DNA project, there's a great deal that you can do to find other results to compare with.

Firstly, most of the testing firms will advertise a free-to-view database of DNA results that they sponsor so that individuals like us can compare our results. In the password-protected web page on the testing lab's website where your personal results are displayed there will generally be an option for you to upload your data into this public database automatically. It is also possible for you to manually input your data, or to search the database without uploading your own data by simply using your own results as your search criteria. Secondly, there may be a website that groups together people with the same DNA signature as yours, or with the same area of geographical interest. This is particularly so for mitochondrial DNA test results where there are interest groups for most of the main DNA signatures, as I'll explain more fully in Chapter 5.

- *Stage seven* is to assess whether the knowledge gained from your results and comparisons has answered your research question(s) set up in stage one. If your hypothesis is fully confirmed, you are fortunate indeed. In many cases, however, it may only be partially or inconclusively confirmed. If this is so, you can consider two broad courses of action: this might be to take a further DNA test (for example at a higher resolution, that is with more markers), or to recheck your documentary research.

- *Stage eight* is basically a process of reviewing your results, and the online databases, from time to time. As the number of test results available for comparison in the online databases increases month by month, so the kind of inferences one can draw from those comparisons deepens and the confidence one can place in them improves. Put another way, the value to you of your DNA test result will continue to increase over time without you lifting another finger, simply because the number of results available for comparison is ever-increasing. Identifying your DNA signature can be seen as an investment that may bring you an additional return at some point in the future!

From time to time you can also review the general genetic testing environment as it may happen that the technology behind the current generation of DNA tests will be improved in a way that makes it advantageous for you to take a new type test when it hits the market.

How to select a testing company

Before reviewing the qualities and offers of the testing companies you need to make two decisions. Firstly, you should decide which type of test(s) you are going to take, as some companies do not offer all types of test. Secondly, if you are taking a Y-chromosome test, you should decide whether you intend to run a surname DNA project yourself in the event that none currently exists.

(Most of the points that follow in this chapter are specific to the Y-chromosome test. Points relevant to the mitochondrial and genetic heritage tests I've placed in Chapters 5 and 6 respectively, where those tests are described in more detail.)

Organizing a Y-chromosome DNA surname study need not be very taxing. Several test companies offer considerable online resources to assist you and the best are able to help you at every step of the way to organize the project efficiently and share the results within your group.

When you're choosing which testing company to team up with consider the following areas:

- the degree of online assistance they can give you to organize the project

- the size of the databases of results they have collected so far

- the costs of their tests, including discounts made available to members of registered projects

- the total number of markers measured in their tests

- their ability to store your processed DNA so that you can have it re-tested later on, if you wish, without having to submit a new sample of your DNA.

Online assistance
As a surname project organizer, the more assistance you can get from a testing company the better. What you need is a mechanism to announce that your project is under way, a method to sign up men who want to take part, a way to collate your results, and a

means to communicate with your group members as you develop the project.

Only one testing company – Family Tree DNA based in Texas – publishes a list of registered surname projects, though all the major firms and labs offering Y-chromosome tests will have some resources available to assist project organizers.

Size of the firm's results database
Clearly it's in your interest as a project organizer to work with the testing company that has the largest possible reference set of Y-chromosome results available for comparison. However, as the people you most want to compare your results with are men who share your surname, I suggest you make a surname search on each test lab's website to see which one has the largest number of name-bearers already registered for the Y-chromosome test. It is in your interest to sign up to a project that already has the largest number of members for your surname regardless of the size of the testing company's overall database of results. If there is no facility for surname searching on a test lab's website you can always search the public databases linked to the major testing labs for Y-chromosome results by surname.

Each of the results found should indicate which testing lab analyzed the original DNA result.

Sadly, it is increasingly common to find not only that new testees are buying the same test from more than one testing company, but also that different people have registered the same surname as a DNA project with different labs. This kind of competition is an exercise in futility as it merely divides the pool of results that everyone needs to make comparisons. If you're tempted to set up a rival project because you don't like the organizer of an existing project, resist that temptation! The only exception to this rule might be where you find a surname project that has already restricted itself to a defined geographical area, for example to just the name-bearers tracing their roots back to the eastern seaboard of the USA. In this case it is legitimate to set up a global project for all surname bearers world-wide.

In all cases the public free-to-view data-bases of results visible on the web, each of which contain a fraction of the results in their sponsoring companies' internal databases, often contain useful Y-chromosome results to compare with.

Test costs and savings

Test companies generally offer lower prices to men taking their Y-chromosome test as a member of a declared surname project. You can register a surname project for your name to access the discounted prices.These cost savings can be significant.

Despite the increasing popularity of DNA testing there are wide differences in prices quoted by the different labs, so it pays to shop around.

It is also worthwhile to watch the exchange rate of sterling against the dollar as the prices offered by non-UK testing firms – which quote their prices in US dollars – can appear to be much cheaper to British genealogists when sterling is strong, as it was in 2007.

Number of markers measured

The greater the number of Y-chromosome markers that you have tested, the higher the resolution your DNA signature will be, and the more confident will be your judgements when comparing the test results in your project to define your genetic families.

Five years ago a 25-marker test was the gold standard for the relatively small number of family historians embarking upon a surname DNA project. Today the same company offers a 67-marker product as its highest-resolution test. Low-resolution tests, typically of just 12 markers, have generally fallen out of use, as there are simply too few markers to define genetic families with sufficient clarity. The experience of the most developed surname-based DNA projects is that at low resolutions the most common DNA signatures appear to lump together many individuals and trees whose documented histories suggest that they are unlikely to be part of a single family tree within a genealogical timeframe. As often as not, when these low-resolution results are expanded by a later high-resolution test, the initial linkage breaks down because the DNA signatures appear, at a higher resolution, to diverge from each other.

Rare DNA signatures, of course, can often stand out even in a low-resolution test, so low-resolution tests are by no means without use. However, it's only with tests of 37–43 markers that the various genetic families will differentiate themselves clearly enough that the results can be used with confidence to direct your documentary research.

Sample storage

Back in the early days, a testing company's offer to retain your DNA sample was not seen as very important. In fact, companies went out of their way to stress that all DNA samples were destroyed after the tests had been conducted. It was felt that people were very suspicious about the potential for their DNA to be misused and that the promise to destroy the samples would allay those fears.

In practice, however, it is very useful if the lab retains your DNA. If the lab improves its tests you will be able to order a new one without having to submit another sample for processing, which is a cheaper and quicker option for you. Secondly, if either you, or your surname project organizer, decide that your result is not clear, and you want to increase the number of markers that have been tested, you can do so more easily by asking the lab to upgrade your test rather than starting from scratch again. Thirdly, it is quite common that another member of your surname DNA group will turn up a DNA signature that is close to yours but not identical. At that point you will be curious to confirm the linkage at the highest resolution possible to find out whether you are related or not, and signing up for that test enhancement is then very easy. Fourthly, and this is a rare case, if there is a query over the result that the lab has produced, the test can be rerun with a minimum of fuss.

In some cases the testing companies have a policy of destroying samples unless you actively opt to have them stored, while in other cases they will automatically retain them unless you expressly request them to destroy them.

*

Details of companies offering each kind of test are to be found in Chapters 4–6 and in the *Useful websites* section at the end of the book. To research more about the different tests and the companies offering them, sub-scribe to a test company newsletter or one of the mailing lists mentioned in the *Useful websites* section.

Chapter 4

Y-chromosome tests

- Haplogroup tests
- Three types of Y-chromosome project
- Solving a problem in your family tree
  Some telling examples
  A note on paternity
- Surname reconstruction projects
  Types of whole-surname project
  A single surname
  Multi-surname projects including variants
  Emigration link-ups
  Taking a wider focus
  Documented whole-surname studies
- Multi-surname projects
  Irish clans
  Scottish clans
  Other types of multi-surname project
- Testing companies and prices
- Online databases

Of all the DNA tests on offer in the market-place, the Y-chromosome test is the most important one for the family historian because its primary use is to help recreate and to check the accuracy of your family tree even though it can only help with one specific line in that tree, the direct paternal line, out of the huge number of lines made up of the many thousands of ancestors of both your parents.

The Y-chromosome test is well established and over the past few decades results have been obtained from hundreds of thousands of individuals around the world. What is not yet clear, though, is some of the finer detail to do with interpreting the results within a surname. Not all the variables associated with the interpretation process have yet been quantified, meaning that your conclusions about your results may involve a degree of uncertainty. A good example is that the exact rate of mutation of each marker has still to be definitively fixed. But even though there is still some debate over the best way to run a project and interpret its results, the guidelines outlined in this book should be robust enough to survive developments over the next few years.

Haplogroup tests

Almost all testing companies nowadays offer a male-line test that is a combination of the standard Y-chromosome DNA test together with an identification of that DNA signature's haplogroup. This is a major improvement on the situation a few years ago when the only way to identify the haplogroup was to buy a separate genetic test. You can, of course, still buy a separate haplogroup test, and I'll explain later why you might want to do that. In any case, however, you do need to be aware of a few issues relating to the format of the combined haplogroup and Y-chromosome results.

The haplogroup test is another name for a DNA test that looks at the one-of-a-kind mutations that migration scientists have used to divide humanity into large groups. In the case of men taking a combined Y-chromosome test, the one-of-a-kind markers that the labs will test to identify the haplogroup (sometimes referred to as SNP markers) are also found on the Y-chromosome, but in different places to the more variable markers (known as STR markers) given as the standard Y-test result.

Haplogoup results are extremely useful because they add another layer of definition to the standard Y-chromosome test result. If you are sorting a large number of Y-chromosome results into genetic families it is very useful indeed to know the haplogroup result for each DNA signature. If one signature is defined as haplogroup R, for example, then it absolutely cannot be related within a genealogical time-frame to another result defined as haplogroup J, even if the two strings of numbers using the standard markers were identical. Here's a simple way to clarify the difference between the two types of markers in your mind: imagine the haplogroup result as defining the *suit* in a pack of cards and the DNA signature as defining the *value* of individual cards. While two jacks or two eights may look much the same, a heart can never be a spade.

Until very recently, if you wanted to find out your haplogroup you had to order and pay for a specific test. Nowadays, the size of the results' databases that most testing firms have built up allows them to associate a specific haplogroup with the majority of standard Y-chromosome DNA signatures. Generally, what the labs will give you will be this inferred identification, not a result confirmed through the DNA testing of your sample. Some of the firms that offer to infer your haplogroup will undertake to run a specific test to measure it if their database cannot offer you an unambiguous haplogroup label. This benefits them because it strengthens their database in the areas where it is currently weak, and it is obviously better for you to have a result that has been tested rather than just inferred. A tested result often provides a higher degree of definition as well as assuring accuracy.

If you want to be sure of your precise haplogroup you can pay the lab to run the separate haplogroup test for you. Generally speaking the labs' inferences can be used as part of the everyday analysis of defining genetic families, but with one note of caution: from time to time, the testing company may decide to slightly downgrade an inferred result that they have already supplied. In extreme cases an inferred haplogroup result may even disappear altogether from your page of results on their website. There's a simple reason why this can sometimes happen.

A particular DNA signature might initially be inferred by the lab as haplogroup R1b1c7 but a few months later appear on the testing firm's website redefined as R1b1. This change suggests that since your result was inferred, another person with the same DNA signature as yours has tested their haplogroup and the result of their test has not been the expected R1b1c7 type but, for example, R1b1c6 or R1b1c5. With this ambiguity newly introduced, the lab has downgraded their earlier inferences for everyone with your exact DNA signature from R1b1c7 to R1b1, the element that the three results all have in common. At this point, if you want to find out whether your own sample really is R1b1c7 rather than R1b1c6 or R1b1c5 then you'll have to pay to take a haplogroup test.

It is thus a good idea to review your haplogroup result from time to time on the testing company's website to check that the lab's inferred identification has not changed. If it has disappeared altogether, approach the lab for a free test to identify it (some labs offer this option). You can also check up on the development of haplogroups in general by looking on the International Society of Genetic Genealogists (ISOGG) and Y-Chromosome Consortium (YCC) websites (the addresses are in the *Useful websites* section).

Three types of Y-chromosome project

There are three main scenarios in family history research that lend themselves to investigation using Y-chromosome DNA tests:

- Solving a problem in your family tree

- Grouping together individuals or trees within the same surname (surname reconstruction projects)

- Linking different surnames within a clan.

You can see that there is a hierarchy of complexity at work here. A problem-solving study is by far the easiest type of DNA project to run, because its goals are generally highly specific. And once completed, you can always expand this kind of project into a whole-surname study at a later date.

Surname reconstruction projects, whether including every bearer of a name or just some of them, aim to develop a matrix of Y-chromosome signatures for all of a surname's family trees. This kind of whole-surname project is the most popular type of DNA project now under way in the family history community. In many cases, the projects that have been registered with the testing labs restrict their focus to specific sub-sets of the surname, usually defined by a geographical area of origin or emigration.

At a higher level still there are a number of

multi-surname projects that have been set up around the world, of which the most convincing are the clan projects. The history of various Scottish and Irish clans links different surnames together within the clan structure, so to understand each clan it makes sense to aggregate individual Y-chromosome results across the full range of potentially related surnames.

In addition, as we shall see later in this chapter, there are a number of declared multi-surname projects that are, for their own reasons, pooling results from many individuals with different surnames, though personally I think that few of these are likely to reach useful conclusions.

By the way, as you read through this chapter you'll notice that a lot of the time I am explaining how you might go about setting up and running a DNA testing project yourself. Most people, of course, won't ever decide to take this step, and there is no requirement that you should. You can simply take your own Y-chromosome test, compare your results with other people's, and leave it at that. But by explaining how you might run your own project I can explain all the issues involved in DNA testing as well as showing how you could move on to the next stage if you wanted to take up that challenge.

Solving a problem in your family tree

Many of the most successful Y-chromosome projects so far were set up to prove or disprove a proposition about a group of ancestors, or to confirm a long-standing genealogical hypothesis that had eluded complete documentation. What one hopes for in this kind of project is that a family tree linkage question that has been frustrating or dividing researchers for a long period of time will be resolved with a degree of closure and satisfaction all round.

The most simple of the problem-solving scenarios is to show that the descendants of two or more men bearing the same surname share a common ancestor. A Y-chromosome test result demonstrating that both men possess the same DNA signature provides the best proof of common ancestry – short of finding the missing documentation – that one could ask for.

This kind of approach can be used to tackle more complicated problems too. Some of the most elegant problem-solving projects have focussed on a specific type of genealogical 'bottleneck' in an attempt to jump across a gap in a family tree caused by missing documentary records. Several DNA studies have, for example, tested the modern-day descendants of a group of immigrants (who have the same or similar surnames) whose ancestors arrived in their new host country at around the same time. Some of these studies have then expanded into a second phase of testing aimed at identifying descendants with the same DNA signature who are still living in the original home country. Looking in both directions, at immigrants and emigrants, the projects build up a matrix of DNA signatures that link families in the New World with their forebears in the Old World.

The problem-solving approach is also a good way to dip your toes in the water. If you don't feel ready to launch a whole-surname project, it's much easier to build up your confidence in the DNA testing process by working with a few researchers seeking to resolve a specific documentary problem or to prove a suspected link between two separate parts of a family tree. Whether you find the answer to their particular question or not, each man's DNA result contributes towards the larger goal of building a matrix of DNA signatures to cover the entire surname.

Here's a summary of some scenarios that a Y-chromosome test might help to solve:

- To prove, or disprove, a connection with a known historical person – e.g. a clan chieftain, a first immigrant, or a famous fellow name-bearer.

- To establish whether two (presently unlinked) family trees are related through a common genetic ancestor within a time-frame that accounts for their shared surname.

- To test a number of people with the same unusual surname in countries of emigration and immigration in order to match together a family in the New World with its ancestral family in Europe.

- To unravel or verify several family trees that may have become jumbled up because several male ancestors had the same fore-names and lived in the same geographical area at the same time.

- To confirm the surname of the suspected father of an illegitimate male child – the illegitimacy having been found in a documented family tree or identified through a DNA surname project – by DNA testing two sets of descendants: those from the father's legitimate family and those of the suspected illegitimate child.

As you can see, these goals cover quite a broad spectrum of research cases. However, in every case the main task is to establish the DNA signature of the target lines accurately and quickly.

You should think about DNA testing several members of each line in order to establish beyond reasonable doubt the authentic DNA signature of the common ancestor at the head of their family tree. Of course, the number of men you need to test increases if the initial results don't match each other as you expected, as can often happen in very large family trees. Once identified, the DNA signature for that tree then acts as a reference result within the project. If someone else signs up later for a Y-chromosome test and finds out that they have this same DNA signature then there's a very good chance indeed that their ancestors link into this family tree at some point.

A programme to link surname-holders in the original emigrant country with their descendants in the New World is really a surname study in all but name. However, in the case of rare surnames where the thesis of the project is that everyone bearing it has a single common male ancestor, it is more logical to promote the project as a quest to find that person.

The fifth case listed above involving a suspected illegitimacy within a documented family tree is much more complicated and is in practice very difficult to resolve satisfactorily. It can be difficult to find two sets of male-line descendants, assuming that they even exist, and to persuade them both to take a DNA test.

Some telling examples
We'll start with the case of a suspected illegitimacy within a tree both because this is a common research situation and because it allows me to outline some important issues that are relevant to all Y-chromosome projects.

In many cases, problematic family trees have an illegitimacy issue at their heart which they hope that Y-chromosome testing may be able to resolve. The crucial factor in this type of project is that a descendant of the man thought to be responsible for fathering an illegitimate child within the main surname's line should be identifiable and willing to take a DNA test to demonstrate the connection.

One DNA project, for the relatively rare

surname of Mumma, had a case like this. In their documented single-ancestor family tree a descendant with the surname Moomaw was recorded with a DNA signature markedly different from the DNA signature for that tree. A review of the documentary research suggested that back in the 1850s his male ancestor had been born to a woman with the maiden name of Mumaw, i.e. his ancestor's father did not carry the Mumma Y-chromosome DNA signature. The child was traced to an entry in the nearest census where he was found bearing the surname Webb. A low-resolution Y-chromosome test was taken by a descendant of the Mr Webb who was also recorded in the house at census time (that is by a male-line descendant of Mr Webb's subsequent legitimate family). The tests revealed that his DNA signature was identical to that of the Moomaw man, thus confirming the documentary research that identified Mr Webb as the probable father of this Mumma child.

While such closure is still unusual, there are many variations on this particular project theme across the family history world. One example is the investigation into the origins of an eighteenth-century American immigrant Captain Daniel Little. It is believed that he hailed from Europe and that he changed his name on arrival in the USA. Several candidates of German origin have been suggested for his Old World identity and tests are under way to check whether any of their documented descendants have the same DNA signature as those of Captain Little in the USA. Finding a connection by this method is a long shot – its hypothesis is less precise than that used by the Mumma project – but it can work.

A note on paternity

All Y-chromosome projects will at some point have to grapple with what geneticists in euphemistic fashion describe as a 'non-pater-nity event'. In the context of genetics this describes the introduction of new male genetic material into an ancestral line by some-one other than the expected male parent – something which might be perhaps more properly called an 'extra-paternity event'.

The impact of this in a surname-based DNA project could hardly be greater. When a num-ber of DNA results for members of the family tree are already available, the interloping genetic material is often so different that it sticks out like a sore thumb. There are occasions, however, when it can look quite similar to the shared

DNA signature, a kind of result that can occur by chance or because the original gene pool was quite restricted (perhaps due to being in an isolated geographical area).

It is also a mistake to think that unusual DNA signatures within your project are the only indication that an illegitimacy event has taken place in your family tree. It can happen that a common DNA signature can mask an illegitimacy event. Also, if it happened a long time ago there may be many modern-day descendants carrying that particular DNA signature as well as the shared surname. Collectively, they might well look like an old and very well-established family tree. (Conversely, a very old family tree might equally well have only a very few modern-day descendants and thus appear to have a very rare DNA signature.)

DNA results do not lie, and if the difference between two DNA signatures cannot be accounted for by change due to the occasional mutation then clearly something else has caused it. However, we should remember that our ancestors chose to change their surnames much more frequently than we might imagine. In many of these cases the documented family trees will appear coherent while the genetic material, when compared across the width of the tree, will look inconsistent.

There were many reasons why, in an existing family, a surname or DNA signature might change, or a new family line be created, and not all of them are shocking. Among these scenarios are:

- an illegitimate son born to an unwed mother, where this male child takes his mother's surname; the child may even be brought up as its grandparents' late child

- a birth within a marriage where the male child is fathered by a man other than the wife's husband, and so inherits the 'wrong' surname

- an infant taking his stepfather's surname on the marriage of his widowed mother and stepfather

- a surname change by the male descendants of a married woman, to ensure that family property is inherited within her maiden surname

- the use of an alias which in time becomes

the main name associated with this particular line, and hence its surname

- personal choice, for example where a man marries an heiress wife and adopts her surname

- where a surname has been badly spelled to the point where it no longer looks anything like the original surname.

Historians don't have accurate estimates about how often each kind of event crops up in the average family tree. Even the average rate of non-paternity is subject to a great deal of argument. One estimate is that in modern-day western societies it could be as high as 5% – or 1 in every 20 births – but some studies put the figure even higher. Most historians generally believe that the rate was not as high as this in medieval times.

So finding a DNA signature that appears to be the odd one out does not necessarily disprove the documentation that links all of the tested descendants together to a common male ancestor. It can, though, be difficult to identify in which generation the slippage in DNA transmission occurred and why. The only

way to find out is to test more male descendants within the tree to narrow down the
options.

From the last few pages it will be clear that
a family historian can have as much, if not
more, fun with a set of non-matching DNA
results as with a set of results that match as
expected. And as so often happens with documentary research, the answers that arise tend
simply to generate new questions. This is
even more the case in the context of whole-
surname projects.

Surname reconstruction projects

The whole-surname project is proving to be
the most popular type of DNA project to set
up, and in many ways it is the easiest type of
project to organize, explain and promote.

Y-chromosome surname projects can be
defined in a number of ways. They can be limited to just a single surname or widened to
include a number of variant spellings. However, the goal of every multiple-surname
project is the same: to identify which of the
many potentially linked or variant surnames do
actually share their genetic heritage.

A central aim of a whole-surname project
is to create a matrix of DNA signatures that

sample descendants from as many family trees within that surname as possible. Such a study can be run for a single surname where no genealogical research has previously been done, in which case the DNA results stand on their own as a guide for future documentary research, or for highly complex groups of surnames where a great deal of genealogical research has been done over a long period of time. But if you are organizing this kind of DNA project you should at all times bear in mind that what the men taking a DNA test really want to know is exactly *how* they are related one to another, not whether they are related or not. In a whole-surname study, the DNA test is just a means towards the end, however distant, of recreating and verifying some well-documented family trees.

It's quite possible that you might start a whole-surname DNA project with no intention of marketing it to potential participants or of working out their documentary history. Your idea might be to register the project and then see who, if anyone, signs up for it. You might wait to undertake and coordinate any documentary research until that point, or you might really only be interested in those people that have the same DNA signature as your own. If so, you'd be in good company as this is what many dozens of DNA project managers are actually doing. But you can still be a bit more proactive without allowing this new project to take over your life completely. And if you are starting a whole-surname project on the back of a first stage problem-solving ancestry project then you already have the makings of a matrix of DNA signatures when you start out.

You will certainly need to prioritize your time as project manager. The single goal you should have in the forefront of your mind is to create a matrix of DNA signatures for the family trees of British origin. If you can identify most of the major British trees by their DNA signature then you are in a very strong position indeed. The appeal of your project will be particularly high to surname holders who live outside of the British Isles, most of whom live in the emigrant-filled countries of the New World, all of whom will be anxious to identify their Old World ancestors. This model holds good for emigrants who settled all over the world in the former dominions in the Americas, Australasia and southern and eastern Africa.

There is also a sound genetic reason why it is a good idea to focus on the British-origin trees first. Because only a small sub-set of the people bearing a particular surname would ever have emigrated from Britain in the first place, and fewer still would have founded successful families in the New World, there is generally less 'genetic diversity' among, say, Americans compared to Britons with the same surname. Put another way, if you were to DNA test a fixed number of men with the same surname in the USA they would be more likely to cluster into a small number of large genetic families than would a similar number tested in the UK.

Despite the theoretical benefits of testing the British trees first, in practice the focus in most projects is usually reversed, for the simple reason that American genealogists have proved more receptive to the idea of DNA testing and are readier to invest in a test at an early stage in their family history research. It is far more common to find a whole-surname project that has a majority of participants with US addresses, and comparatively few British-origin results, than the other way round.

As you can imagine, organizing a whole-surname project is a long-term commitment. Participants will join every year, but the scale of most surname projects is such that no organizer of one based on a common surname is likely in the near future to declare that its DNA testing programme is closed because its DNA signatures are so well defined, and its documented family trees so clearly corroborated, that further testing is not needed. On the other hand, the number of participants that is needed to create a useful matrix of DNA signatures for a surname may not be as large as you think.

The number broadly depends on how rare your surname is and how many variant spellings you are including in the project. By sampling around 5% of adult males in Britain you should be able to create a matrix of DNA results that will serve as a reliable tool to identify the major genetic families in your surname. For many surnames this means as few as a dozen or so men need to be tested. And if you are patient you can easily run such a project in a low-key manner, waiting for interested people to find it themselves and join up, rather than actively pursing potential project members.

As the DNA signature matrix for your surname takes shape it will gradually become clear whether your surname is more likely to have had a single male ancestor that you all share or whether it was founded by multiple male ancestors at different times and in different places.

One thing to bear in mind is that only a few relatively rare surnames will ever look from the very beginning of the project as though they are of single-ancestor origin. It is much more common, especially with any surname with more than, say, 1,000 bearers alive in the UK, that the distribution of results will always make it appear to have a multiple ancestor origin. We are collectively still in the early stages of working out what the ratio of single- and multiple-origin surnames really is, and the answer won't become clearer for some time. Anecdotal suggestions are that some surnames start to take on more of a single-origin pattern as the number of participants in their project increases and the number of documented trees associated with the sur-name is reduced due to successful research, but there are no figures yet to demonstrate this.

While many potential participants are likely to find the chance to prove that they belong to a surname that has a single common ancestor quite appealing, you can promote the multiple-ancestor scenario to them on the grounds that by taking a Y-chromosome test they can hope to find some new relatives to fit into their family tree.

Types of whole-surname project

At its simplest level, a DNA surname project consists of aggregating DNA signature results from as many men as possible with the same surname and analyzing the patterns of connection – by building up genetic families – that emerge. This process usually produces immediately useful results because the genetic families reveal previously unsuspected links between members of different family trees and suggest further lines of documentary research.

While a worldwide study of a unique surname is the simplest type of surname-based DNA project to promote, there are a number of different elements and stages that can be incorporated into it to develop its potential. These include:

- tracking a single surname in a specific geographical area

- exploring variant or foreign versions of the principal surname as part of a multi-surname study

- focussing on countries of emigration and immigration

- widening the study in specific ways, e.g. to include all surnames categorized within the main surname's Soundex category (Soundex is a system that links surnames based upon how they sound when spoken)

- integrating the DNA project with a documentary family tree reconstruction process.

You'll notice that many of these surname projects chime well with the different types we looked at earlier as problem-solving ancestry projects. In fact, the distinction between a problem-solving project and a whole-surname project is not always precise, nor need it be. As a DNA study collects more and more results it will inevitably start to look like a fully fledged surname study even if that wasn't your original intention!

A single surname
The family trees of very common surnames are extremely hard to research in a traditional way even in a single country let alone on a global basis. The number of surname-bearers is simply too great for them to be linked together

using a traditional documentary approach with any confidence of completion. In these cases Y-chromosome testing offers a unique way forward simply because it links participants into genetic families with a high degree of confidence. Each genetic family represents just a fraction of the total number of people bearing the surname. But once segregated into these smaller groups anyone tackling the documentary research can start it with a greater hope of eventual success. In effect, the DNA results have created a series of mini documentary research projects within the same surname.

The other way to tackle the problem of a very common surname is to restrict the DNA project to one geographical area. For example, rather than launch a worldwide project for a surname that accounts for more than 1% of all men of British origin, one Smith surname project is tracking only Smiths who believe that they originate in the southern states in the USA, while a partner project covers the northeastern states. These two projects appear to have access to each other's results, but if they did not then one risk would be immediately apparent: put simply, some Smiths might sign up to the wrong project. If, for example, your origins were in the northern states, not in the southern states as you'd thought, then your initial choice could prove a costly waste of time as you'd be comparing your result with the 'wrong' matrix. This simple example underlines a fundamental aspect of surname DNA projects: rival projects only dilute the pool of results available for comparison.

Multi-surname projects including variants
Many DNA projects are built around a group of surnames that have equal status with each other even though some are more common than others. For example, the Pomeroy study includes several linked surnames – Pomroy, Pomery and Pummery – that are found today in Britain and that have links to the same geographical areas of origin as the dominant spelling of Pomeroy. Our project also includes two other surnames that are today found only outside the UK, a surprisingly common feature among surname projects in general: Pommeroy in Australia and Pumroy in the USA.

With this kind of multiple-but-linked surname project it helps to handle the results in two ways at the same time. On one level of analysis you should treat all results as equal in status and impact regardless of whether they belong to the dominant spelling or to a variant.

In fact, having made this point, now is as good a time as any to emphasize that it is best practice always to review a group of DNA results initially in isolation, without referencing the other data relating to their trees, so as to avoid the risk of your judgement being skewed by hopes and expectations.

Having looked at all the data by lumping together all the different spellings into a single big matrix of DNA results, you can later review the results by individual surname to see if any patterns of difference stand out. In many cases such patterns will indeed be visible.

From my own project I can confirm that the genetic families created by the Y-chromosome results include many trees that contain men with different variant surnames. This demonstrates something that genealogists know only too well, that the spelling of a surname is an unreliable guide when reconstructing family trees. Or to put it another way, surnames have a very much higher rate of mutation than our Y-chromosome DNA!

In fact, the spelling issue is more complicated even than that. In my own project we know from our documentary research that certain spellings are more common in particular

English counties: for example, Pomery is the most common spelling in Cornwall whilst Pomeroy is the most prevalent in neighbouring Devon. Of course, the surnames in many of our families have altered over the centuries, a process which has generally seen the introduction of the dominant modern spelling of Pomeroy into families that trace back to a differently spelled ancestor.

When our DNA results are overlaid on the data documenting the origin of our family trees, a very interesting story emerges. In contrast to the Pomeroy trees, the modern-day bearers of the less common variant of Pomery link back only to a very small number of documented families, all of which stem from Cornwall and not from neighbouring Devon. What the DNA results then add is that these trees look as though they might have a single common ancestor while the trees bearing the other spellings of Pomeroy and Pomroy do not.

Emigration link-ups
There are several types of surname-based emigrant/immigrant project under way around the world. They range from standard whole-surname projects with a declared focus on New World/Old World linkages to more

complex projects trying to uncover different possible connections between countries.

This style of project is increasingly popular in the USA where many project organizers are looking at surnames that were introduced into North America by multiple immigrants and where 'surname naturalization' has occurred regularly as foreign names, from a range of different European languages, have been anglicized upon entry.

A good example is the Cooper study which includes the variant spellings of Couper and Cowper from Britain, Coupard and Cuopard from France, and Cuper, Keefer, Kieffer, Kifer, Kueffer, Kupfer and Kupper from Germany.

The linked surnames can either be brought into the study on the basis of a semantic linkage – for example the German and French equivalents of the English profession of 'cooper' – or because they sound like the English surname Cooper and might plausibly have been adopted by immigrants to the USA for that reason.

Most surname projects will find examples of this kind of adaptation if they dig deep enough. Despite our West Country origins, the wider Pomeroy family in Britain, which has its roots in the Norman Conquest of 1066, has two Pomeroy trees headed by Russians who changed their name from Pomeransky when they came to London a century or so ago.

Taking a wider focus
Many research groups find it a challenge to identify the boundaries between different potential variant surnames that they might include in their study. Some adopt a narrow focus to define their DNA project whilst others range more widely.

Many advanced surname projects find that they have to include other surnames in their project as it grows in order to check whether the DNA record suggests undiscovered links. Some projects adopt a wide embrace from the outset.

The Bracewell project includes a range of surnames that begin with the letter 'B' and sound like 'dazzle'. It reports that identical DNA signatures have been found in men with such different surnames as Braswell, Brazell, Brazil and Bracewell, showing that some might share a common ancestor within a surname-relevant timeframe despite the apparent disparities between their names.

Documented whole-surname studies

The gold standard among Y-chromosome projects is the amalgamation of genetic and documentary results for a whole surname. This combines data from the Y-chromosome test with the well-developed resources of a long-term worldwide documentary family tree project.

This kind of integrated surname project is extremely difficult to achieve and very few completed or near-complete studies yet exist. Their starting objective is to reconstruct all the family trees associated with the surname, and any linked variants, and then to DNA test at least two modern-day descendants from each of those family trees to establish conclusively each tree's DNA signature. The resulting documentary research aims to resolve all of the genetically linked trees in each genetic family into a single documented family tree, which will then be verified by its consistent set of DNA results.

This coordinated process is potentially extremely powerful in its reach, using the DNA results both to corroborate cherished family trees and to knock holes in their long-accepted documentation.

To give a sense of the scale of the task

facing such a surname research group we can look at one active and well-organized Y-chromosome project under way run by the Pennington Family History Association. This group has data on more than 16,500 house-holds worldwide, roughly one-fifth of which are in the UK. The 69 Y-chromosome results they have collected so far reveal firstly that several distinct families have adopted the sur-name Pennington over the years – i.e. it is a multi-ancestor surname – and secondly that all the documented families that have held the surname for many centuries probably link back to just one or two villages in Lancashire in north-east England. The researchers have even demonstrated a connection with several men bearing the surname Radcliffe, evidence which may corroborate a story about one ori-gin of the Pennington name, which documents how the family of Margery de Pininton, who married a Hugh de Radcliffe in 1220, adopted the surname that became Pennington.

The mountain facing this kind of all-embracing project is simply that documenting all the potential family trees is very time-consuming and hard to complete for any surname other than a relatively rare one. But as more and more basic genealogical data become available on the internet, the number of such projects will rise and those under way will move closer to completion. While progress can seem very slow, a progression does take place. Back in 2000 when the research group I now coordinate started grouping modern Pomeroys living in Britain into family trees, we found over 300 trees, mostly comprising very small numbers of individuals. Seven years later, after absorbing the knowledge gleaned from DNA testing and researchers' documentary delving, the number of trees has fallen to well below 50. The DNA evidence now suggests it will eventually fall below 30 and that perhaps as many as two in five of all name-bearers in the last 500 years belong in one single large family tree.

So few surname reconstruction projects have reached completion that it is too early as yet to comprehend the full impact they will ultimately have on family history studies. The importance of DNA testing in this context is that it is the crucial tool that confirms the accuracy of the documented trees, and thus of all the conclusions drawn from them. Results from this kind of project will one day also have major implications for studies of the origins of surnames and provide huge insights into the ways we have devised of classifying and understanding them. But that is still some way off.

Multi-surname projects

There are many DNA studies tracking Irish and Scottish clans that are beginning to produce interesting results. These projects pool together results from the wide group of surnames that have historically been associated with each clan. The results of these studies will reveal whether the different surnames traditionally associated with each clan do in fact share the same genetic heritage.

Irish clans

The Irish clans' study has grown out of an academic testing programme using the genetics lab at Trinity College, Dublin, sponsored by a member of the Guinness family. Its initial findings, reporting the results of more than 1,000 tests across 43 surnames, indicate that some well-known surnames appear to stem from a single common ancestor, as I'll explain in detail in Chapter 7.

Another paper using data from this project revealed linkages among surnames believed to have been associated with the Ui Neill, the most important dynasty of early medieval

Ireland. It found that about one in five males sampled in north-west Ireland was a likely male-line descendant of this specific early medieval ancestor, another reminder that the full power of DNA testing to reveal the hidden links between surnames has yet to be felt. In this case, the DNA results confirmed the stories of a number of semi-mythological early Irish genealogies.

Scottish clans

The Scottish clans' project takes a different approach. Run by a group of non-academics, it is collecting the Y-chromosome results from anyone bearing a surname with a Scottish connection. DNA testing looks as though it may one day resolve a series of historical debates about Scottish clans and their lineages.

Clans in Scotland originated in the kin groups of the Picts and the native Scots, which were later overlaid with feudal obligations and subsequently associated with the clan chief or laird who was in turn known by the name of his chief estate. The exact features of clan and kinship are often debated and Professor David Hey notes in *The Oxford Companion to Local and Family History* that a clan was 'a unit that contained families of different lineages;

common descent is often assumed but cannot be proved ... Chiefs, like the barons of England, were indifferent to whether or not the people over whom they ruled shared the name and blood.' Long-term conflicts between clans sometimes led to entire clan names being erased from public life across several generations, so a single lineage might change its surname more than once in a way that simply didn't happen south of the border.

All of which might lead you to expect that DNA results from among the Scottish clans would be a bit mixed up. But Professor Bryan Sykes recently conducted Y-chromosome tests on members of the MacDonald clan – including five clan chieftains – with the goal, as he relates in his book, *Adam's Curse,* of identifying the Y-chromosome of their purported common ancestor, a twelfth-century chieftain named Somerled. Ironically, the DNA signature that the professor identified as Somerled's is common in Scandinavia, leading him to suspect that the ancestor of a man often described as being historically related to the kings of Ireland was, in fact, of Norse or Viking genetic ancestry. Given an estimated number of two million male MacDonalds worldwide, Professor Sykes speculates that as many as

400,000 of them could have 'Somerled's Y-chromosome' some 36 generations later.

Other types of multi-surname project
DNA study organizers have come up with a number of variations on the basic theme of the surname DNA project. In most cases the idea has been, like the Scottish clans project, to aggregate the results across a large number of surnames in order to examine a particular hypothesis.

Two studies that stand out focus on specific geographical areas of Britain: Wales and the Shetland Islands. The Welsh used a patronymic naming system – where the father's given name is passed on as a surname – until relatively recently, so the history associated with Welsh surnames is comparatively less developed than in England. But DNA testing can identify a shared heritage that cuts across the genetically jumbled surnames to reveal a history based on DNA signatures held in common.

A second project is reviewing the DNA – both Y-chromosome and mtDNA – of men with links to the Shetland Islands which lie in the far north of Scotland. It is investigating whether men with Norse-origin names – such as Williamson, Anderson or Thomason – have different types of Y-chromosome signatures compared to men with Scottish surnames – such as Leask, Bain or Mur.

A number of other multi- or cross-surname projects exist that are defined by characteristics other than geography. One example is a project investigating the genetic inheritance of members of the Chitpavan – or Kokanastha Brahmin – an Indian community numbering slightly over half a million or a fraction of 1% of that country's total population. Less than three centuries ago this community was strictly isolated in a small area in the state of Maharashtra. Today it recognizes several dozen surnames as typical of its caste, which now form the criteria for inclusion in their project.

Testing companies and prices

The number of companies offering Y-chromosome tests seems to grow every year. There is a benefit in using a testing company that is well established, so I'll outline here only the three leading firms. For a longer list of all the firms please see the *Useful websites* section at the end of the book.

The market leading firm is Family Tree DNA,

based in Houston, Texas. It uses the lab of Dr Michael Hammer at the University of Arizona to conduct its tests. It has the widest database of Y-chromosome results available for comparison of any company and it claims to host nine out of ten of all Y-chromosome surname projects currently under way around the world. It sells tests ranging in resolution from 12 to 67 markers.

Family Tree DNA has two main rivals. Relative Genetics, based in Salt Lake City, Utah, is now closely allied with the owners of the Ancestry.com stable of genealogical websites. It runs its own ISO-accredited DNA testing lab, in effect running the entire process inside the company. It offers tests ranging from 18 to 43 markers.

In the UK, the most established firm offering the Y-chromosome DNA test is DNA Heritage, based in Weymouth in Dorset. It uses the lab facilities owned by Relative Genetics to perform its DNA tests. This firm offers a standard 43-marker test, though you can increase the number of markers or reduce them to a minimum of 23.

I've outlined in Chapter 3 how you might set about choosing which test company is right for you.

It is always worthwhile to review the prices offered by the test companies, both to individuals seeking a test and to members of a registered surname group. Such is the competition between companies that they actively encourage you to set up a surname group and access the discounted price even if you are currently the only person coming forward to take the test. Average prices have dropped during the past few years. For registered groups the lowest-resolution test (around 12–18 markers) now costs less than US$100. A medium-resolution test (around 25 markers) can be found for around US$150 and a high-resolution test (37–43 markers) for less than US$200. The highest-resolution test, the Family Tree DNA 67-marker test, costs US$269 within a group project and US$349 outside of one. (At the time of writing in mid-2007 you could figure that a pound sterling was worth two US dollars.)

Online databases

Don't forget to have a regular look at the various online databases of results. The three leading test companies have each set up a public database on the web where their own clients can automatically upload their results and make them available to public view. Another useful resource is the Y-STR mapping site which generates maps showing the present-day distribution of low-resolution Y-chromosome DNA signatures. Addresses for these databases are in the *Useful websites* section at the end of the book.

"Pears"

Chapter 5

Mitochondrial DNA tests

- All about Eve
- How the mtDNA test differs from the Y-test
  The underlying genetics
  The test results
- Uses of the mtDNA test
- Mixing results
- Testing companies and prices

So far in this book the spotlight has primarily been on the Y-chromosome test and its ability to reveal the paternal heritage of the men taking it. The test that reveals our direct maternal heritage, the mitochondrial DNA test, stands as its poor relation only because the lack of a tradition of maternally transmitted surnames makes it less easy for family historians to use the test on a regular basis to solve problems in their family trees. However, one plus point is that the mitochondrial DNA (or mtDNA) test has been used by population geneticists for more three decades. So it is well established and well understood, with a large number of results available for comparison.

All about Eve

One of the scientists' early conclusions using the mtDNA test was that all of us alive on earth are descendants of a single woman, who is often dubbed our mitochondrial or ancestral 'Eve'. Unlike the biblical Eve, she wasn't the only woman alive at the time when she herself lived. What's significant about her is that none of her contemporaries produced any modern-day descendants. Put another way, Eve was the only successful mother of her time, if we measure success as producing female off-spring that in turn produced female-line descendants alive today.

There is, of course, a single ancestral 'Adam' to all of us as well. As with Eve, what's unique about him is that he is the only man of his time who has any male-line descendants. And unlike the biblical Adam, our ancestral Y-chromosome Adam did not live at the same time as our mitochondrial Eve. She may have lived as long ago as 200,000 years before the present while Adam lived perhaps as recently as 60,000 years ago.

The picture of our single common maternal ancestor has been slightly muddied by the most popular book on the subject, *The Seven Daughters of Eve* by Professor Bryan Sykes. His choice of seven mitochondrial ancestral types is somewhat arbitrary. The one feature the seven had in common is that they were not 'daughters' of 'Eve' in anything other than a loose metaphorical sense, as they all lived thousands of years' apart. The 'maternal clans' that each one represents have no significance for family historians either.

How the mtDNA test differs from the Y-test

We already know that mitochondrial DNA is different from Y-chromosome DNA in its pattern of transmission: both men and women inherit their mitochondrial DNA signature from their mothers.

The underlying genetics

The genetics behind the mitochondrial DNA test are different too. Mitochondria are tiny pieces of genetic structure crammed inside every cell in our bodies. Unlike the 46 chromosomes in our traditional DNA, which transmit data from one generation to the next, the vital job performed by mitochondria relates to the energy management of their host cell. Their basic function is to use oxygen to take energy out of our food, but a simpler way of thinking of them is as a kind of battery for the cell.

This description may not sound particularly promising for family historians, but for our purposes the role of mitochondrial DNA is insignificant: what matters is that we inherit its genetic pattern from our mother, as she inherited it from her mother, and so on back in time – so the passing down of the mitochondrial DNA signature follows the direct maternal line in exactly the same way that the

Y-chromosome test follows the direct paternal line.

Mitochondrial DNA doesn't just have a different cellular role to that of Y-chromosome DNA: it is structurally different too. Mitochondrial DNA is arranged in a circle rather than the coiled-up double helix of the chromosomes: the two ends of the DNA string join up. Scientists have agreed by convention that their measurements of mitochondrial DNA should always start in the centre of what is known as the 'control region' (or HVR), which appears to have a role in the mitochondrion's replication process. As this region doesn't carry the vital data being replicated – which is found in the 'coding region' – chance mutations can occur without causing the replication process to fail. It is these mutations – inherited over time by successive descendants – that make comparisons between samples useful, though they are relatively very few in number compared to the mutations seen within the Y-chromosome.

The test results
Another key difference is in the way the test results are presented. The mtDNA result that you get back from the testing lab does not look

like the standard Y-chromosome string of numerical values. Instead it summarizes the differences between your mtDNA result and that of a designated reference result known as the Cambridge Reference Sequence (CRS) using a series of letters. The historical reason for this is that mitochondrial DNA was first sequenced (in Cambridge, England, in 1981) from an anonymous woman. The CRS is her test result. After years of subsequent mitochondrial data collection and comparison across the world it turns out that she held one of the more common patterns of mitochondrial DNA found across Europe today. Note though that the CRS result is not the most common mtDNA result found in any particular population in Europe today, nor is it that of any mitochondrial Eve (or even one of Eve's seven daughters). The choice of the individual now immortalized as the CRS was purely fortuitous; the result itself is not special or typical in any way.

When you take a mitochondrial DNA test you'll find that each testing lab selects a section of the HVR for testing and comparison against the Cambridge Reference Sequence. Scientists are working hard to improve the degree of resolution offered by mitochondrial

DNA results, and testing companies already offer mtDNA tests that investigate both the non-coding and coding parts of the mitochondrion. In future, we can expect that tests for the entire sequence will start to be offered at a price level appealing to a wide range of genealogists.

One feature that is unlikely to change, though, is the potentially confusing way that mitochondrial DNA results are described. As with Y-chromosome results, mitochondrial DNA results are classified into haplogroups. Unfortunately, these haplogroups are labelled by capital letter (e.g. H or L) in an exactly similar manner to Y-chromosome haplogroups. Unfortunately there is no connection between the Y-chromosome haplogroup classified as 'R' and the mitochondrial DNA haplogroup defined as 'R'. It is very easy, when reading up haplogroup descriptions on the internet, to mistake mtDNA haplogroups for Y-chromosome haplogroups, and vice versa.

One of the disadvantages of mtDNA results arises from the fact that the average rate of mutation of mitochondrial DNA is very much slower than that of the Y-chromosome. This means not only that pinpointing *when* a particular mutation occurred is very difficult, but also that it almost certainly happened a long time ago. One upshot of this is that if you compare your mitochondrial DNA result with everyone else who has ever taken the test you are pretty much guaranteed to find others with exactly the same result as yours. However, you are less likely to be able to identify whether the direct maternal ancestor you share lived relatively recently or even tens of thousands of years ago. Looking for a documentable connection will most likely be an exercise in frustration. Even more so than with the Y-chromosome test, when using the mtDNA test as a genealogist you need to start with a hypothesis about a particular maternal connection, and then to use the test to support or challenge it.

Uses of the mtDNA test

Compared to the Y-chromosome test, the genealogical uses of the mtDNA test are limited and highly specific. But if it is technically possible to use the mtDNA test to confirm your particular hypothesis then it can be an extremely powerful tool.

As the test can only be used in relation to the direct maternal line, the two people being tested have to believe that they share a common direct maternal ancestor. With the

Y-chromosome test any same-surname match will be useful – you can leave it to your documentary research to find out later exactly how that man is your relation. But with the mtDNA test no such latitude is possible; your research has to be accurate throughout the two lines being tested for the mtDNA test to be able to deliver you a positive result. While Y-chromosome testees can go on a 'fishing trip' to look for matches, the mtDNA testee is highly unlikely to find any relatives by chance.

With the Y-chromosome test it is very easy to identify people to compare your result with: they are all the men with your surname. With the mitochondrial DNA test, identifying the pool of potential test partners is a very different and time-consuming process. The proportion of family historians who are prepared to research such remote cousin relationships is only a very small percentage of the total: many wish only to research their tree back a few generations, or to recreate their paternal line tree, where the shared surname is such a great help in tracking relationships. So while the mitochondrial DNA test is potentially very effective, my feeling is that its usefulness to the average family historian is quite low. On the other hand, for those researchers who are dedicated enough to do the groundwork into these remote relationships, the mtDNA test can be uniquely effective.

One application might be to prove, by testing their direct maternal line descendants, that two women were sisters (or maternal cousins). Another case might involve testing the descendants of the daughters of two brothers in cases where you are not sure which daughter was born of which mother; if you can find a direct female line descendant from the disputed daughters, plus a direct female line descendant from each of the two wives (whose mitochondrial DNA results will be different to each other's), you will be able to identify the correct mother. Another case might be the situation of a man with multiple wives where the birth date (and therefore identity of the mother) of a female child is unclear; again, one would need to test a direct female descendant of each of the potential wives as well as of the child to reveal the true mother.

Just looking at these mitochondrial DNA test scenarios reveals that they are generally more complex than the typical Y-chromosome scenario. They also tend to relate to more modern genetic links, back just a few generations, as it is so much harder to research maternal lines further back.

One area where a mitochondrial DNA test can deliver strong benefits is in cases where there is no option to document family links within the standard genealogical timeframe, for example where the documents simply never existed. The deep ancestry link that the results can reveal is of much greater value to a researcher if he or she cannot find new information about their origins in other ways.

One example is someone who believes their maternal lineage traces back to a slave forcibly brought from Africa to the USA. In such a case the paper trail might run out one or more generations after that female ancestor was brought to the Americas, leaving their origins in Africa completely obscure. Nowadays a mtDNA test result can be matched against a global database that includes results taken throughout modern-day Africa, which can pinpoint a region or country in Africa where the same mtDNA result is found today. As migration patterns in Africa are broadly known in the period of the last 500 years, the ancestral motherland associated with that particular mtDNA result can be identified. In effect, the mtDNA test has found that descendant's maternal homeland.

In some cases a mitochondrial DNA test is

used to determine a family link so close to the modern era that it ends up functioning in the manner of a maternity test. The website of the International Society of Genetic Genealogists cites one example that illustrates this point rather well. The case describes a woman whose mother had been adopted, an adoption that supposedly covered up her illegitimate birth. A detailed mitochondrial DNA test of someone thought to have been the sister of the adopted woman came back with an exact match with the adopted woman's daughter, confirming for the first time the identity of the adopted woman's birth family.

Mixing results

The most common question that I get asked about DNA testing invariably involves the questioner's desire to verify a relationship that lies somewhere in their family tree other than along the direct paternal or direct maternal lines. Surely, they ask, it is possible to combine a Y-chromosome test result and a mitochondrial test result in order to find the answer they seek?

Alas, the answer is no: results from the two tests cannot be combined together, they can only ever be used to compare like with like. And as you'll by now have understood, no other ancestral link apart from the direct paternal and direct maternal lines can be tested using these two available DNA tests.

Testing companies and prices

The list of firms offering mtDNA tests is the same as that for Y-chromosome tests at the end of Chapter 4. Pricing ranges from around US$125 for the lowest-resolution test up to US$495 for Family Tree DNA's fullest test. Some test companies offer discounted prices to men who have already taken their Y-chromosome test.

Chapter 6

Genetic heritage tests

- The Genographic Project
- The range of heritage DNA tests on offer
- Issues with heritage tests
  Kinship tests
  Tribal tests
  Geographical heritage
- Companies offering heritage tests
- Invented histories

'Heritage' DNA tests come in a variety of shapes and sizes. Some of these are built upon the two techniques I've already described – the Y-chromosome and mitochondrial DNA tests – while others use a different kind of test altogether, as I explain below. The key point about all of them, however, is that their results are generally not part of a family historian's toolkit: you cannot expect them to be of any use to you as you try to reconstruct your family tree. But they certainly offer insights, sometimes interesting ones, about one aspect of your origins, and the timeframe they address reaches further into the past than you can through genealogy.

That's a pretty major caveat, and you may well ask why I'm including them in this book which is aimed at helping family historians to get the most out of the opportunities offered by DNA testing. One answer is that almost every testing company that offers the standard genealogical DNA tests will also offer a range of heritage DNA tests, so it's useful to understand what they are. A broader reply is that the value of this kind of test depends on your personal appreciation of history and where its meaning lies for you. I'm the kind of person who likes old documents and statistical detail, and as yet I haven't found these tests interesting enough to buy one. But you may feel that the insights they promise are highly meaningful for you – many family historians these days are interested in their distant past as much as in adding names to trees – and I wouldn't want to pooh-pooh that response at all.

As with the standard genealogical DNA tests, the quality of the heritage DNA tests is improving over time, so I may in future have cause to change my mind about them. And, as I shall explain, there are a small number of people whose family trees are for perfectly valid reasons well-nigh impossible to reconstruct, for whom the insights these tests offer will always have a special compensating significance.

The Genographic Project

The growth in popularity of heritage tests is one of the outstanding features of the past few years in the changing field of DNA testing. Symptomatic of this growth is the huge international popularity of the Genographic Project, sponsored by The National Geographic magazine and IBM. Begun in 2005, it is a global undertaking that hopes to identify in great detail the migration paths of all humankind over tens of thousands of years. Due to run until 2010, the project has two main targets: firstly, to test the DNA of 100,000 indigenous people from around the planet in order to record the high degree of diversity in their genetic make-up; and secondly, to encourage anyone else who wants to participate to buy a test kit and contribute their anonymous results to the project's collective database. To date tens of thousands of people have responded to that call, men for a 12-marker Y-chromosome test and women for a standard mitochondrial DNA test, making the Genographic Project the largest genetic testing undertaking of its kind.

The project is run by a recognized authority in the field, Dr Spencer Wells, and there's every sign that the project's database will grow to such a size by the close of the programme that its outputs will provide definitive answers to all the key 'big picture' questions about the origins of humanity. It should certainly give a clearer picture of the main pathways taken by humankind to spread around the planet, and in doing so it may answer some long-disputed questions about associated timeframes and chronologies.

You can join the Genographic Project by

applying to it directly, or by taking a test with a company called Family Tree DNA and associating your results with the Project's database. Bear in mind that if you go through Family Tree DNA you gain the genealogical benefit of taking part in a surname DNA project and receiving a set of results comparable with other surname-based results. If you join the Genographic Project directly you won't receive any kind of personal result back that will allow you make such comparisons. You can, though, elect to join a surname project on Family Tree DNA, which will allow you to view your own and matching results.

The range of heritage DNA tests on offer

The obvious attraction of popular science and the idea of DNA tests for the masses that is at the heart of this kind of large-scale DNA project have led testing labs over the past few years to create several new kinds of heritage test designed to tap into this appeal, so let's spend the rest of this chapter looking at some of their offerings.

The key feature about almost all of the heritage DNA tests is that they promise insights into your deep ancestry, that is into your genetic origins in the timeframe prior to your genealogically verifiable history. In other words, they aim to tell you something about your ancestry in the period of time since the end of the last Ice Age up until the time that genealogically useful records started to be kept. Some tests focus on the more recent end of that time period, as I'll explain, in an attempt to create a story that can become part of the prologue to your family history.

In scope and promise the tests vary widely. Starting with the timeframe they target, some are focussed on a relatively modern period such as the first millennium of the Christian era while others take a longer look back to the last Ice Age or try to plot a particular migration route out of Africa.

Some of the tests seek to establish kinship with a specific historical person, for example, to the fifth-century Irish clan chief, the head of the Ui Neill known as Niall of the Nine Hostages; or to the twelfth-century Scottish warlord, Somerled, King of the Hebrides; or to the thirteenth-century Mongolian invader of Europe, Genghis Khan.

Some tests try to infer a particular tribal origin, to interpret your genetic make-up in a way that identifies you with a particular tribe or group of people. A popular example that several companies offer is a test to link you to the Picts of Scotland or to the Vikings of Norway.

Another set of heritage tests take a different approach entirely. They interrogate a wider spectrum of your DNA, all the DNA found in your cells excluding the sex-determining chromosome and mtDNA in fact, in an attempt to give you an overview of your overall genetic make up. The results from these autosomal DNA tests are presented to you as a percentage breakdown by the geographical region of genetic origin. For example, your result might say that your genetic heritage is 83% Indo-European, 12% Sub-Saharan, 4% East Asian and 1% Native American.

Issues with heritage tests

Each of the types of test described above has problems associated with it. For me those problems outweigh the potential benefits, but you may feel differently.

Kinship tests
Let's start with the 'kinship tests', the ones that link you with a particular historical individual. These tests use the same Y-chromosome test that we've already seen performing as a

genealogical tool. The new twist involves the testing companies interpreting the currently understood pattern of Y-chromosome DNA signature distribution across the British Isles and Europe. Where a particularly common DNA signature is found that coincides with the history of a dominant individual, the assumption is made that the DNA signature belongs to that person because this is the most likely explanation for its modern-day dominance. There's a logic behind this, as one of the principles of genetics is that a common DNA signature represents a set of genes that has been successful in perpetuating itself. It's logical to expect that a socially dominant individual would have had lots of male children who in turn would have had lots more themselves – but that's not quite the same as genealogical proof. Within our family histories, genealogists know that the most widespread family today is not necessarily the oldest.

Another point to remember is that famous people do not have unique DNA signatures. In many cases they are likely to have been born into a community with a fairly restricted gene pool. The DNA signature associated with Genghis Khan was surely held by other men in Mongolia, and it is reasonable to expect that as the armies of the first Great Khan spread west they came with them alongside their leader. So it is certain that some men in present-day Europe are descended from one of the fellow travellers, from the third archer from the right on the back row, rather from the Great Khan himself. To put it another way, the DNA signature reveals the common stock you're from, but it doesn't prove descent from an individual.

I once met an American who told me he was related to the Soviet dictator Josef Stalin. What he meant was that one of his recent Georgian forebears shared Stalin's surname. Just for fun I told him that I was related to Stalin too, and also to Hitler, which caused him to pause for a moment. I'm also related to you, dear reader, both on my father's line and on my mother's, for the simple reason that everyone on earth links back to a single male and a single female ancestor. What's important in this case is the matter of degree. Compared to the history of humanity 1,000 years seems a very short time indeed, but in terms of the mixing of our genetic heritage it is long enough to link a great many of us together.

Matt Ridley gives a very good example of how this mixing process works in his book *The Red Queen*. He points out that 1,000 years ago, the passing of just 30 generations, my extended family tree would theoretically contain over one billion ancestors. You can calculate this yourself, going back generation by generation and doubling the number of ancestors (2, 4, 8, 16, 32) 30 times until you reach this huge number. Of course, the population of Britain 1,000 years ago was only a tiny fraction of a billion people, which means that my extended tree starts to contain more and more duplicated ancestors in each generation the further I go back. Ultimately we really are all related; it's up to each of us to decide at what point our shared kinship becomes relevant or important.

Tribal tests
The 'tribal' DNA tests make similar leaps of faith as the 'kinship' tests. Today you can take your own standard Y-chromosome test result and then go online to check the distribution of that DNA signature across present-day Europe. The map that appears on your screen records the places where that DNA signature has been found in the past few years in test programmes undertaken by bona fide academic testing labs. Now let's say that your particular DNA signature has been found many times

in Scandinavia and sometimes in Britain, but is much less common in Spain and Portugal. This kind of distribution could be explained as one consistent with a Viking heritage, but it does not prove that your ancestor was an actual Viking, someone who got on a boat and went plundering.

I regularly lecture on DNA testing to family history societies around Britain, and one example I use to illustrate this problem is to put up a slide showing the map of a particular Y-chromosome DNA signature distribution that is typical in modern-day Europe. The map shows a strong cluster of results across modern Sweden and Norway, and virtually none along the western Atlantic seaboard. It's the kind of distribution that looks to the eye to be distinctively Scandinavian. As with my example above, one is immediately tempted to project it back in history 20 generations or more and describe it as typical of a Viking heritage. On this broad-brush level that's a reasonable assumption; the problems arise when you look at the detail.

On the map there is one location that stands out, right on the bottom right-hand edge, in modern-day Istanbul. Here a single example of this particular result has been found. The map tells us nothing about the identity or history of that person, only that an individual tested recently in Istanbul was found to have that DNA signature. At this point, I tell the audience, one can start imagining how this typically Swedish haplotype (DNA signature) made its way to Turkey. Perhaps, we can suggest, that it belonged to a strapping Viking who made his way down the river from Kiev to become a member of the Varangian guard in imperial Constantinople a millennium ago? And just as that romantic thought is lodging itself in their minds, I remind them that it could equally have resulted from the visit of a wimpy Swedish match salesman a century ago who achieved no success in the city but to leave, without his certain knowledge, his Y-chromosome behind. There's not even any assurance from the map that the owner of the DNA found in Istanbul, or his ancestors, had any connection with Sweden at all.

The tribal tests use the modern-day distribution of a DNA signature as a proxy for a particular heritage. In some cases they base their connection on specific values in a tiny number of markers, a very low-resolution DNA signature indeed. In many cases, the identifications claimed are not yet backed up by a published scientific paper, so there's no way to check exactly how the link is being made. And while many associations are bolstered by a level of statistical analysis, there are still many unknowns that are just estimates in the calculations, not least the mutation rate of individual markers.

While there is no genetic test for any particular tribal identity, as few tribes appear to have had a pure enough stock to be so clearly identified, it is possible to say that some DNA results are consistent with a particular history. A recent television series in the UK, *The Face of Britain*, got around this difficulty by telling the people it tested that their result was, for example, five times more likely to be associated with a Norse Viking heritage than an Anglo-Saxon one. That kind of qualification is very important if your interest is in history rather than fantasy.

It's hardly surprising that few tribes have a strong genetic identity, as the movement of peoples around Europe and to and from Britain has been very active in the past few thousands of years. To take the example of the Vikings, these invaders came from two main areas: one group from the north, the Nordic Vikings, the other from the south, the Danish Vikings.

The northern Vikings have DNA signatures that stand out strongly across the British Isles and in the islands of northern Scotland. The Danish Vikings, however, came from roughly the same area as the homeland of the Saxons, the tribe that they fought to displace in England. Historically the two groups are quite different; genetically they cannot be told apart. The Danish Vikings also colonized along northern France, thus mixing their genetic heritage with the people who later became the Normans who famously came to Britain in 1066. It would be wonderful if the genetic heritage of these three groups, not to mention the Jutes, the Angles and Picts from around the same period, could be individually unravelled, but alas there is no genetic test that distinguishes between the invading Normans, the defeated Anglo-Saxons (of all types), or the Danish raiders of earlier generations. One group that is relatively visible is the original population of Britain dating back before Roman times. But as roughly two-thirds of all Britons, including myself, possess this genetic heritage it doesn't really add much to one's genealogy.

Geographical heritage

A third type of heritage DNA test looks at the DNA of all of your 46 chromosomes, and it faces a different set of problems. As I mentioned earlier, the results from this kind of test are presented to you as a percentage breakdown by the geographical region of genetic origin (e.g. 83% Indo-European, 12% Sub-Saharan, 4% East Asian and 1% Native American).

The main issue here is one of degree again. The percentage breakdown figures are only claimed to be accurate to within a few percentage points for each of the geographical categories. If you recall the calculation we made of the number of our ancestors we each have 1,000 years ago you'll remember that just five generations back we have 32 ancestors, each one of whom represents – averaged out – around 3% of our overall heritage. So in practice, you almost certainly won't see any unusual genetic heritage you hold (for example, that long-lost American Indian relation) if the ancestor(s) in question entered your tree further back than six or seven generations ago.

Of course, if your result does come back strongly weighted towards one of the geographical areas defined by the test in a way that you did not expect, or cannot account for, then you can try working out why that might be so. The DNA result itself, however, will not give you any indication which of your many ancestors is responsible for the result. Your best bet is to ask your father and mother to take the test to see whether the unusual result is reflected in one of them in particular.

To summarize, it is safe to say that none of the tests mentioned in this chapter will advance your genealogical research; except in a few very rare cases, they will not help you to document the family tree that defines your genealogical links to your closest ancestors. Secondly, none of these tests will confirm your descent from a particular historical person; only your genealogy can do that by documenting the precise link between the two of you across the generations that divide you. They can associate you with a shared genetic stock, but they can't prove your descent from a specific individual.

Clearly many people find meaning in their heritage DNA test results otherwise the testing companies would not still be offering them. What they actually mean to you, as an individual, depends on where you find meaning in your own history. For me, these geographic and kinship DNA tests don't offer enough insight into my past to justify the cost of gaining the result, particularly when our knowledge of Y-chromosome DNA signatures now includes an indication of my deep ancestry history since the Ice Age. Compared to the benefits created within a complex surname reconstruction project, a fancy certificate telling me I'm by origin a Celt tells me very little indeed.

Companies offering heritage tests

With those caveats in mind, the rest of this chapter reviews the leading testing companies and the range of heritage tests they offer.

Family Tree DNA

US-based Family Tree DNA is the market leader in the area of surname-based Y-chromosome tests. It does not offer heritage DNA tests per se, though it does flag when a Y-chromosome result tallies with a known historical haplotype. So it will indicate if your result matches the Ui Neill ancestral DNA signature that has been identified by researchers at Trinity College, Dublin. It will also flag up potential connections for samples within Jewish, African and Native American contexts. The firm's clients can donate their DNA results directly to the Genographic Project's anonymous offline database via their personal web page.

DNA Heritage
British-based DNA Heritage, despite its name, does not sell heritage DNA tests, though you can buy a Y-chromosome haplogroup test from them.

Relative Genetics
US-based Relative Genetics, now linked to My Family Inc and the growing family of Ancestry websites, does not perform heritage DNA tests itself but resells those provided by a firm called DNA Print Genomics (see below).

African Ancestry
African Ancestry is a US-based firm run by academic Dr Rick Kittles which uses a proprietorial database of African samples he has built up from more than 30 countries and 160 different ethnic groups using data from published sources, research collaborations and primary research. In mid-2007 it contained 11,747 paternal lineage samples and 13,690 maternal samples. Its data are not in the public

domain. The firm's ability to review African-origin DNA samples is unmatched by any other firm, but one fact to bear in mind, as shown a few years ago in the television documentary *Motherland*, is that roughly 30% of male African Americans carry a European Y-chromosome haplotype.

Oxford Ancestors

A British-based company set up by surname genealogy pioneer Professor Bryan Sykes. It uses its own classification of 15 Y-chromosome 'clans' that correlate 'with a probability of up to 97%' with the haplogroups defined by the body that oversees the developments in this field, the Y-Chromosome Consortium. The firm also offers to interpret Y-chromosome results to differentiate between 'the Celts, the Anglo-Saxons/Danish Vikings and the Norse Vikings'. Its website does not explain how these classifications are made. Clients receive a certificate showing the 'most likely tribal origin' of their Y-chromosome plus 'information about your ancient tribal ancestors and insights into their life and times'.

Oxford Ancestors offers mitochondrial DNA tests which are still classified according to the 'seven daughters of Eve' as outlined in

Professor Sykes' 2001 book of the same name.

Ethnoancestry
A British-based company, run by geneticists, that offers a number of heritage DNA tests. It advertises the following Y-chromosome 'types': Irish 'Niall of the Nine Hostages', Scottish 'Lord of the Isles', Mongolian 'Genghis Khan', Chinese 'Manchu dynasty', Jewish 'High Priest' type, Norse Viking, Scottish Pict. Its website does not explain how the classifications in these tests were arrived at.

The firm also offers Y-chromosome tests that will differentiate men into the roughly 50 male clans identified in Stephen Oppenheimer's recent book *The Origins of the British*. These clans do not correspond to the haplogroups defined by the Y-Chromosome Consortium and are based on results that have not yet been made public.

The firm advertises a future 'total genomic ancestry test' available for both men and women that will reveal the percentage ancestry based on 'different continental groups – African, Native American, East Asian, Pacific Islander and Western Eurasian'.

DNA Print Genomics

A US-based firm that markets a range of heritage tests including a basic autosomal test dubbed *AncestryByDNA* as well as Y-chromosome and mtDNA haplogroup tests.

A follow-up autosomal test dubbed *EuroDNA 2.0* uses 1,349 markers. This test reports your 'proportional basic continental European ancestry' in the following categories: south-eastern Europe (Armenian, Jewish, Italian and Greek), Iberian (Spanish, Portuguese), Basque (Spanish/French Pyrenees border), Continental European (German, Irish, English, Dutch, French, Swiss and some Italian) and north-eastern European (Polish, Baltic, Swedish, Norwegian, Finnish, Russian). The firm cites a recently published scientific paper as the first to effectively resolve the distribution of European populations based on autosomal markers including the five 'fundamental and ancient types of European ancestry' above. Its website claims that rival tests use less meaningful markers and too few of them while their own test 'is the only legitimate genomic autosomal test for sub-European ancestry' based on published, peer-reviewed work.

The firm recently acquired another heritage

test lab called Trace Genetics. Its tests are marketed by other firms such as Relative Genetics, Genebase and Genetree.

DNA Tribes
This US-based firm offers a patented statistical analysis of your autosomal test results that 'compares your genetic profile to a population database that includes over 193,000 individuals from 655 populations around the world, including 467 indigenous populations'. The result, it claims, benefits by being based upon observed results. However, it also notes that 'a match with a particular ethnic or national population sample does not guarantee you or a recent ancestor (parent or grandparent, for instance) are a member of that ethnic group'. Despite the statistical rigour deployed the report produced remains loaded with qualifications. The sample report for a 'Caucasian' on its website concludes, for example, that 'Catalan would be the most likely population of origin, but other ethnic origins such as Flemish, German or Italian cannot be excluded. It is also possible this individual could be of Irish or French heritage.' Despite its name, its results don't reveal your 'tribe'.

Geogene
This US-based firm markets two heritage tests, one called *GeoFather* which samples the Y-chromosome and the other called *GeoMother* which samples mitochondrial DNA. These appear to be standard haplogroup tests.

*

The arena occupied by genetic heritage tests is complex, rapidly changing and, I would argue, only of peripheral interest for most genealogists. If you want to keep up with developments in this field I recommend you check the International Society of Genetic Genealogists (ISOGG) web page that monitors them: www.isogg.org/eochart.htm.

The cost of these tests ranges from around £65 for a haplogroup test to as much as £340 for a combined Y-chromosome and mtDNA analysis.

Invented histories

While DNA tests are peripheral for most family historians, they can still be fun. A recent one-off television programme in Britain titled *100% English* conducted autosomal DNA tests on six people who announced confidently that they considered themselves to be pure-blooded Anglos. They included a well-known right-wing politician and a leading light in a small national-ist party. Without explaining how the test worked in any detail, the programme took that metaphorical sense of a pure English identity and pulled the rug out from under the partici-pants by showing them that there is no such thing as pure English genetic stock. Race, in a genetic context, doesn't mean much; it's a purely social construct.

Fictionalizing and romanticizing are danger-ous pastimes in conjunction with history. Bryan Sykes' *Seven Daughters of Eve* set the ball rolling in the DNA field with its potted biographies of seven women complete with appropriate emotional repertoires. If your pulse beats a little faster at the prospect, as the professor's website says, that the 'heroic Y-chromosome that flowed through the veins of the High Kings of Ireland' might also filter through your own, then this kind of genetic test is for you.

After this DNA detour, in the rest of this book I'll look at the kind of results that family historians have unearthed in their Y-chromo-some and mitochondrial DNA projects, and explain how you might select a company to test your DNA and to help you organize your own project.

Famous DNA

Related to Genghis Khan

Approximately 16 million Asian men can consider themselves descendants of the great Mongolian warlord Genghis Khan. This finding by an international team of researchers was confirmed when a cluster of closely related lines, fanning from a common ancestor, was found within several thousand Y-chromosome samples taken throughout central Asia. Analysis showed that the cluster originated in Mongolia about 1,000 years ago, while its distribution across Asia coincided with the boundaries set by the Mongol Empire in the same period. About 35% of Mongolian men share this DNA signature.

The *Titanic* baby

An early success for historical DNA testing was chalked up in 2002. For years the baby buried in a small plot in a cemetery in Halifax, Nova Scotia, a victim of the *Titanic's* demise in 1912, was known poignantly as the 'unknown child'. Eighty years later Canadian researchers identified him as a 13-month-old Finnish boy, Eino Viljami Panula. But another five years later, they revealed that they had got it wrong, and further tests showed that the infant was a 19-month-old English boy called Sidney Leslie

Goodwin. Dental evidence which had inclined the team towards the Finnish boy has now been conclusively overturned with a new set of enhanced DNA tests.

The lost colony

DNA testing is being used to tackle the greatest unsolved mystery in the history of America: what happened to the 'lost colony' of Roanoke Island in Virginia, which disappeared without trace in 1590? Roanoke was set up in 1587, nearly two decades before the more famous successful first colony of Jamestown. Its founder, John White, left to return to England, promising to return with supplies within three months, but the threat of the Spanish Armada delayed his return for three years. Today's researchers are focussing on a nearby area where many surnames match those on the roster of the former colony. Almost 50 linked surnames will be checked in a long-term project that will probably include descendants of the original colonists living today in the UK.

Christopher Columbus: gentleman or pirate?

Spanish scientists are using DNA testing to find out if Christopher Columbus, who famously landed in America in 1492, wasn't the Italian gentleman of conventional history but in reality a former pirate born in Catalonia. They are comparing the results of Y-chromosome tests taken from hundreds of Catalans surnamed Colom with results of a sample taken from Columbus's illegitimate son Hernando, whose remains lie in Seville Cathedral. While most historians have accepted that Columbus was an Italian born in 1451 in Genoa, others passionately argue that the international mariner was really called Cristofol Colom.

The Russian royals

The identification of the bodies of the Russian royal family, executed during the 1917 revolution, was only finally proven as the result of DNA evidence from modern-day royalty. The remains of Czar Nicholas, Czarina Alexandra, three of their children, their physician and three servants were mixed together and unrecognizable when they were found in a shared grave in Yekaterinburg. The evidence came from a sample of mitochondrial DNA taken from Prince Philip, the husband of Queen Elizabeth II, who shares a direct maternal ancestor with the dead Czar.

Thomas Jefferson, founding father

American historians had long debated whether one of the founding fathers, Thomas Jefferson, had indeed fathered children by one of his black slaves, Sally Hemings – until DNA testing came up with the evidence of connection. A question mark still hangs over the conclusion, however, as records show that several other Jeffersons in his family, who carried the same Y-chromosome DNA signature as Thomas, visited the family home at Monticello and could therefore have fathered one or more of Sally's six children.

Chapter 7

Some success stories

- Davenport
- Steadham
- Hurst
- Kerchner
- Creer
- Meates
- The Irish clans
- Mitochondrial DNA

Hundreds of thousands of people have already taken a DNA test, and with the results of several tens of thousands of those tests visible on the internet it's fair to say that a wide range of family history scenarios has already been the subject of genetic examination. This chapter gives you a flavour of some of the success stories that people have reported in their quest to verify their family trees and discover new relatives. What you'll notice is that in many cases the genealogical breakthrough was due to a happy coincidence. This typically comes about when someone takes a DNA test and finds that their result connects them with someone else who has the missing piece of documentary research they've been seeking for years.

Bear in mind too that this chapter is about successes. It's easy to forget that some people who have bought a DNA test didn't find the answers that they were looking for. I don't want to be alarmist by pointing that out. Most people realize quickly enough when they start researching their family history that the truth they uncover might not tally with the stories that have been handed down the generations. And as with documentary research, DNA research can come up with ambiguous answers as well as unexpected or even unwelcome ones. If that thought is of concern then you might want to find another hobby before the frustrations of genealogy overwhelm you!

I've arranged the stories in this chapter so that the simpler ones are at the beginning and the more complex ones towards the end. As you read through you'll get a sense not just of how DNA testing might help you but of the range of complexities and subtleties associated with the interpretation of the results and the organization of DNA projects. The International Society of Genetic Genealogists (ISOGG) has a web page that collects similar accounts, and that's a good place to read up on more stories like these. Let's start by looking at some Y-chromosome project examples.

Davenport

This surname project is a good example of how a targeted Y-chromosome DNA project can build upon several generations of documentary research to confirm a family history that has been accepted for some time but not proven. It is also a very good example of how to conduct research on both sides of the Atlantic, and of how Old World families in

Britain and those of emigrants in the New World can be brought together.

The Davenport surname has been traced back in England to before the Norman Conquest in 1066 AD. The oldest documented individual, one Ormus de Davenport, lived in the Cheshire area in north-west England. As with many long-established surnames, a particularly dedicated nineteenth-century researcher spent many years creating a detailed genealogy going back through those 800 years. It was this story that the Davenport DNA project set out more than a century later to confirm or to challenge.

As happens with many projects, the initial interest in DNA verification was sparked in the USA. The Davenport surname has a long connection with the colonies of the eastern seaboard, notably through the Reverend John Davenport, the founder of New Haven, Connecticut. Researchers had identified no fewer than five Davenports residing in the Boston area in the early 1600s: the Reverend John, Thomas, Humphrey, Captain Richard, and Lancelot. All five reputedly came from England and shared the same family crest, but any genealogical link that could connect them had long been lost. Could the DNA results corroborate that missing documentary evidence?

Within a year of commencing the project had shown that descendants of the Reverend John, Thomas and Captain Richard shared a common ancestor. Their common result also matched those of descendants linked to another Richard Davenport, also born in England, who had settled first in Virginia and later in North Carolina. With this genetic family established and now linking together the majority of American-born Davenport descendants, the project turned its attention to Britain and began a search for Davenports with a Cheshire ancestry. A few early results linked to that area also matched with those of the large American-led genetic family, thus broadly confirming the nineteenth-century research. The high point of the project came when one of the very few lines that can document its claim back to Ormus de Davenport came up with the same DNA match.

Steadham

This DNA project is in essence similar to the Davenport one, but with a tighter focus. The common ancestry being tested stretches back not ten centuries to Norman England but just three to seventeenth-century Delaware in the eastern USA. The methodology used was the same as in the Davenport surname project, though the focus in this case was to prove a specific ancestry rather than to undertake a surname-wide matching process.

The Steadham project is led by Richard Steadham, whose family stems from Alabama. He co-founded the *Timen Stiddem Society*, a family association linking together the descendants of a seventeenth-century Swedish barber surgeon, who settled in New Sweden – now Wilmington – in Delaware, and his five sons. Richard's primary concern was to check which of the many documented descendants of the barber could be genetically confirmed, and secondly to identify which modern-day descendants bearing the surname of Stidham or Steadham – or any of 15 others thought to be variant spellings – are genetically linked to Timen Stiddem.

His results revealed that nine male family members with documented histories linking them to three of Timen's five sons have near-identical DNA signatures and all belong to the same unusual haplogroup. A further four men who are documentarily linked to a Samuel

Stidham do not share this DNA signature. Samuel was originally believed to be related to a Scot who emigrated to the USA called John Steedman, but the DNA results suggest that this is not so. Even more surprisingly for Richard, one of John Steedman's long-documented descendants is revealed genetically to be a descendant of Timen Stiddem instead.

With 42 results collated, this project, now in its seventh year, holds a highly useful matrix of data that it can use to link new men coming into the programme and which is still generating new insights about which of many variant surnames are linked and which are not.

*

The power of DNA testing to reorganize years of archival research can be seen time and again across a great many projects, as can the kind of unexpected linkage that proves a particular connection and overcomes years of frustration at the failure to find the right supporting documentation.

A good example comes from the Fuller surname DNA project. It reports that it has two participants whose families both tell the story that they are descended from Plymouth Pilgrims who arrived in the USA on the

Mayflower. Neither man has, however, been able to get their documentation back far enough to cover the first few generations after the boat's arrival in Massachusetts in 1620. When their DNA results came back from the lab they showed that not only do the two men share the same DNA signature, but that their results also match that of another member of their DNA project who has constructed a paper trail of descent from a *Mayflower* passenger named Edward Fuller.

Another story, this time from the Hart DNA project, reveals the delight one American felt when he found that his DNA signature matched that of the descendants of Stephen Hart, who arrived in Massachusetts from Essex in England with his wife and children in 1631. This news stimulated him to start researching his family history in detail. I've noticed this trait before in other projects. Many people who want to know about their origins often don't feel the urge to set about researching them. But when their DNA result arrives suggesting a match with someone they've heard about in their history, that revelation not only directs the focus of their future research, it also creates a strong incentive for them to put time aside to research it.

Of course, the reverse experience – genetic proof of non-connection – also often occurs. Of the 100 Pomeroys tested in my own project not one has so far come up as an exact match with the DNA signature of the modern-day descendant of the noble family which in Norman times owned manors all over Devon and Somerset. Everyone in the wider family has heard of this family and the castle at Berry Pomeroy, but none of us can show a genetic connection with it.

Hurst

The Hurst DNA Project provides a slightly different example of how a small project can develop into one with far-reaching implications. Hurst is a very common surname, and it makes sense to start any surname-wide project of this scale with a smaller challenge before broadening it out to take in all comers. In this case the project started out with the aim of resolving a specific question about two families in a single eastern American state, but once it had done that it simply carried on and progressed to test – and then overturn – a long-held theory about the Hursts' purported origins in England.

The project got off to a good start when the

first four men tested turned out to have the same 37-marker DNA signature. Two of them link back to an individual born in 1750 in Virginia while the other two link to another family in a nearby part of the same state. Some time ago a respected genealogist had concluded that these two families were not related, a judgement that the DNA evidence has now clearly overturned.

Like the Davenports, the Hurst surname also has a nineteenth-century historian in its ranks. This person had put out a theory that one of the Virginia families was descended from a family found in the English parish of Leckhampstead in Buckinghamshire. This theory had since been broadly rejected by English genealogists but the story is still believed by many American Hursts. The DNA results, taken from three Hursts descended through that Buckinghamshire line, proved to be completely different from the genetic family containing the Virginians, confirming that the original story linking them together was a red herring.

This kind of scenario, where history has to be rewritten, is very common. Not all of us are as lucky as the Davenport family, who had a reliable nineteenth-century historian writing up their history, and the reluctance of many members of the Hurst family in the USA to give up on their Buckinghamshire link is echoed in many other projects including my own. I think of these 'false histories' as a kind of genealogical virus. In my own case the false trail was created almost a century ago by an American genealogist who managed to link the largest and most well-documented Pomeroy family tree in the USA to the English nobility by the simple act of inventing a 'missing' baptism record in an early parish register. Many bearers of the name still hold to the belief that they have some connection with the noble family, based upon a book now a century old that cited this false research, but the DNA results show that there is no connection at all.

Kerchner

This project illustrates why it is a good idea to use high-resolution Y-chromosome DNA tests rather than rely on the less expensive low-resolution ones.

The project is led by one of the early adopters of genetic genealogy, Charles Kerchner, and from the outset had several goals. Firstly, Charles wanted to confirm traditional research which suggested that two immigrants who arrived in Pennsylvania, Adam Kerchner in 1741 and Frederick Kerchner in 1751, were closely related; and secondly to see whether bearers of several variant spellings were genetically linked to the more popular spellings of the surname.

In its early days the project suffered what appeared to be a setback. It was easy enough to find a pair of descendants of both Adam and Frederick to test. And while each pair of descendants came back with consistent DNA results, the problem was that the two sets were different from each other. As a pioneer, Charles was using the best test available at the time, which was a low-resolution test of just 12 markers. The two sets were different from each other on two of these 12 markers, a difference that five years ago was seen as indicating that the two lines could not share a common ancestor within the past several hundred years. However, since that early assessment was made the testing environment has improved and higher-resolution tests have come on the market. No new documentary evidence had been found to disprove or doubt the earlier conclusion that Adam and Frederick were related, possibly even as siblings, and so Charles decided to re-test the original sets of samples using the newer, improved tests. If the two sets of descendants were truly members of two different family trees then one would expect their results to diverge further from each other as the resolution of the test increased. What happened was quite remarkable. Testing at 25 markers the two sets of results matched on 23 markers; no further differences were found compared to the 12-marker test. Later still they were re-tested again and found to match on 35 out of 37 markers. The two sets of results, which had started out looking so different, had ended up after testing at a higher resolution instead looking very much as though they shared a common ancestor.

Charles also made use of a calculation available to researchers to determine the date when his samples shared their Most Recent Common Ancestor (MRCA). If this equation sounds as though it could provide all the answers to your own family history dilemma then take a deep breath: it is not quite as useful as it sounds. What the MRCA calculation does is to estimate the number of generations back in time that two men shared their common ancestor. It does this by looking at the differences between the two DNA signatures and working out how long ago those two strings of results could have been identical, i.e. what length of time would have needed to elapse for the two strings, once identical, to have accumulated the mutations needed so that they look as different as they do today. It is important to understand that the MRCA calculation can only ever provide a very approximate answer to the often vital question – when did the common ancestor live? – because there are so many variables in play, many of which are unclear. So for example while the number of markers used in the calculation is important, the truth is that we still don't know for sure how those markers behave when they mutate. The mutation rate of each marker is not precisely quantified as yet. Furthermore, the result of the calculation is expressed in terms of the probability that the common ancestor fell within a particular timeframe, and it can't be made any more specific or accurate than that. For example, it may say that there is a 90% chance that two men share a common ancestor who lived 15–21 generations ago. This kind of vagueness is generally very frustrating for a genealogist who would dearly love to get the kind of answer that says 'The common ancestor was born in 1327.' In practice, the MRCA calculation is only sometimes as useful as its title suggests, and more often than not this happens when it is being used to look at faraway linkages – for example, in a clan project where the common ancestor might have lived according to legend some 800 years ago – rather than in relation to relatively modern lineages. (To find the calculation online, look in the *Useful websites* section at the end of the book.)

Charles though was able to use the MRCA calculation broadly to back up his linkage thesis. His conclusion was that Adam and Frederick probably did share a common ancestor who might conceivably have lived about 300–360 years ago. His current thesis is that the two immigrants might have been cousins of some kind, or uncle and nephew. This would account for their shared surname, their settling in the same area, but also for the absence of any church or legal records suggesting an intimate interaction between their two families, as might be expected had they been brothers. It's a useful thesis to direct further research in Germany: the assumption that they might have come to America from the same village or locality.

Charles is still looking to find the original

Kerchner male line in Germany, though his results show that the Kershner and Karchner surnames are related to Kerchner as suspected.

This connecting of different but related surnames is a feature of many well-developed DNA projects. A few also report surprising connections as asides to their main lines of enquiry. One example from the MacLaren DNA Project, a surname associated in its history with the surname Lawson, records that one of its Lawson participants came up with a match with someone outside of their project surnamed Losson. The suggestion is that this match is accounted for through an unusual, and relatively modern, name shift from Lawson to Losson. It's the kind of link that almost certainly would not have been found without the spotlight of the DNA test result to highlight it.

The more developed the documentary research behind a DNA project, the more exciting its results can be. The last few examples show just how powerful the combination of the two types of research can be.

Creer

Anyone bearing the surname Creer is doubly fortunate. Their name has been extensively and carefully studied by a member of the Guild of One-Name Studies called John Creer, and the Y-chromosome results associated with it confirm that the roughly 1,000 bearers of the name worldwide today form part of a single family tree and hence link back to a single Creer ancestor. John's analysis of the oldest available documentary records reveal the presence of several Creer families living in a valley on the Isle of Man, situated between Ireland and England. Back in the sixteenth century the family name was McCrere, a form typical of most Manx Gaelic family names at that time in its use of the prefix 'Mac', the Gaelic word meaning 'son of'. Within a century or so, again in common with most other Manx names, this prefix had fallen out of use and the surname was rendered simply as Creer.

John's aim in setting up his Y-chromosome project was to get around the lack of documentary evidence in the period prior to around 1600. With his detailed knowledge of the different Creer family trees, John was able to find male Creers to take a DNA test who were living in the Isle of Man, and in England, the USA, Australia and Canada. The 22 men selected each had a documented history going back at least eight generations, roughly to the mid-1700s.

The results were clear. Seventeen out of the 22 men tested recorded DNA signatures that were so very closely grouped together that they could be described as descendants of an original 'ancestral Creer'. The trees represented by these 17 testees include at least half of all Creer men alive today.

And if the central finding – that all Creers from the Isle of Man are related – isn't impressive enough, the project has uncovered still more news. The remaining five results recorded DNA signatures that were markedly different from that of the ancestral Creer. One of these was unexpected, as that particular tree was headed by an illegitimate male birth where the boy had taken the surname Creer after the 'father' named by his mother. The DNA result for his descendant, however, suggests that he his father was not a Creer after all.

Note that the presence of the five non-matching DNA samples doesn't mean that the Creer surname has to have multiple origins. Even though almost a quarter of the men tested have a different DNA signature, the documentary evidence still links them into the main Creer family tree. In many surname DNA projects even if half of all the DNA results collected are different from the modal result one can still describe the surname itself has having a single genetic origin because we can expect that most of the differences found can be explained away as illegitimacies like the Creer example given above that have accumulated over many generations.

Using the MRCA calculation John was able to show that the ancestral Creer probably lived in the century and a half before the year 1400. Another clue about his origin was revealed by the haplogroup of the DNA signature of the ancestral Creer, which is classified as the R1b1c type. This is typical of the oldest inhabitants of the British Isles rather than of later invaders such as the Vikings or Saxons. While many men from the Isle of Man might expect to find their DNA suggesting a Viking origin, the original Creer could easily have come from somewhere else. There is some evidence to suggest that the name McCrerie existed in nearby Galloway in Scotland in the fifteenth century. So did the ancestral Creer come over from Scotland? The Isle of Man was under Scottish rule at various times in the period between 1200 and 1400 and is a short sail from Galloway. The DNA evidence seems to hint at the possibility of this connection.

John's conclusion is that the DNA analysis

has answered, very persuasively, a question that it has not been possible to solve hitherto by using conventional genealogical research. This study clearly demonstrates how this new technique does really work in conjunction with existing genealogy research and can bring new and powerful insights. It has unblocked a major barrier that was stalling the Creer family history. In addition, all Creers are now provided with a new sense of a common identity and family – and genetic clues are available to help track the history of that family even further back than the fourteenth century.

Meates

Some DNA projects become so detailed that they open up completely new areas of research that were never contemplated by the project manager when testing was started. Another Guild of One-Name Studies member, Susan Meates, has experienced this several times in her project, which started with the simple goal of finding out whether everyone with her surname had a common male ancestor. She already knew that five trees had their origins in Ireland, one other in the English county of Worcestershire close to the Welsh border, and another in Wales itself. Frustrated by the absence of records that she could use to link together the Irish trees earlier than the late 1700s, she saw that DNA testing offered a new way to bridge that documentary gap.

The initial results were very illuminating. When someone in every family tree bearing the surname Meates had been tested, the results revealed that all the Irish trees fall into a single genetic family while the Worcestershire and Welsh trees each have different DNA signatures.

Susan then turned her attention to the other surnames, including Meats, Mates and Mate, all long thought to be linked, that she'd been researching as part of her documentary project. The results she found created a new level of understanding for her. Every Meats family tree, all the Irish trees for Mates bar one, and several Mate and Mates family trees that trace their origins to counties in England and Wales, all broadly matched the DNA signature of the Irish Meates' trees.

Her attention now focussed on understanding the whole process of surname evolution, Susan started to include several surnames that she'd originally not thought of as potentially linked to her own, including the much more common surname Myatt. When the DNA results started coming back the picture became clearer still. All the Myatt family trees that she could find to test, bar one, matched with the Irish Meates genetic family.

After further documentary research, Susan now believes that all these surnames descend from the surname Mayott, which originated in north Staffordshire, not far from Worcestershire and the Welsh border, and is first visible in a document dated 1281. In common with most other surnames visible 700 years ago, this single surname was spelled in many different ways. (In fact, it's a feature of old documents that you can often see references to a single person spelled in several different ways in the same document: consistency of spelling was not a virtue until much more recently!) However, only some of those variant spellings ever became established enough to propagate family trees of their own. While spellings such as Meot and Mete never got established and do not survive in the present day, Meate arose some time in the 1500s, and Meates some two centuries later. In fact, based upon the DNA results and documentary evidence that Susan has collected, it looks as though the surname Meates evolved on at least three separate occasions, in Ireland, Worcestershire and Wales. The root surnames they evolved from may well have been different too.

One neat feature of the DNA results when comparing one genetic family with another is that there may well be a distinctive value on one specific marker that all the members of one such 'family' share that is slightly different from that of the other 'family'. By looking across the whole spectrum of results it becomes possible, using the same principles as the migration scientists use to arrange haplogroups in their order of formation, to work out which value of the marker is the original or ancestral value and which other values have been created through later mutations. In Susan's study, all the participants from Irish Meates trees share one such distinctive marker value. This shared genetic heritage suggests that their common ancestor lived after the progenitor of the surname and that those called Meates form a separate branch off the ancestral Mayott tree.

Susan's project has led her to do a great deal of detective work around the world to trace down descendants of some of her family trees that have no known descendants living in Britain. The Meates tree from Worcestershire, for example, today only has members living in Australia and Fiji. Similarly, all the Meates living in New Zealand are members of just one of that surname's family trees. So far Susan has enrolled participants in her DNA project from 16 countries including France, Belgium, Switzerland, Romania, Moldova, Australia, New Zealand, South Africa, Canada, Fiji, Singapore, Thailand and the USA.

Susan's study also alerts us to the danger of assuming that finding multiple DNA signatures means that the surname being studied must have had more than one original ancestor. She points out that several centuries can elapse between the time that a surname is adopted by one individual and the year that most family trees can be traced back to; plenty of time for a genuine single-ancestor surname to accumulate some different DNA amongst its members. The key to understanding the history of a surname is to use DNA testing and documentary research together to track its evolution.

The Irish clans

My final Y-chromosome example is the most well-developed surname-based study conducted anywhere in the world to date. Led by academics from Trinity College, Dublin, it set out to investigate the genetic history of several dozen Irish surnames. The results it found were somewhat surprising as several surnames, ones so common that you and I have almost certainly met someone bearing them, turned out to be of single-ancestor origin.

Ireland has used surnames in the way we do today, passing them on from father to son, for even longer than the English have: indeed some Irish surnames appeared as early as the tenth century. Many of these surnames also have a great deal of history – some of it so old that it is purely oral – in the form of stories that link different surnames together into clans. By testing a range of surnames, researchers hoped to check the truth of these histories as well as to subject the theory of DNA testing in relation to surnames to the most comprehensive examination it has ever faced.

Forty-three surnames, including six of the top ten most common surnames in Ireland, were selected for inclusion in the project. A total of 1,125 men submitted their DNA sample for analysis with each sample being tested on 17 markers.

The most encouraging conclusion, for all of us, was that the programme demonstrated once again the power of Y-chromosome DNA testing to unearth a previously hidden genetic heritage for many of the surnames tested. Further to that, the headline results showed that on average, a man in the programme had a 30-fold increased likelihood of sharing the same DNA signature with someone of the same surname compared to someone else with a different name.

Perhaps astonishingly at first glance, surnames such as Ryan and O'Sullivan – both with around 30,000 bearers in modern Ireland – were found to have a pattern of DNA signatures that strongly indicated a single original ancestor while other surnames like Murphy and Kelly – the two most common surnames in Ireland, each with around 65,000 bearers and representing more than 1% of the entire Irish population – clearly appeared to have multiple ancestors. Both of the latter surnames are thought to derive from personal names believed to be common centuries ago. This would account both for their widespread nature across the country and for the broad range of DNA signatures associated with them today.

Irish surnames are particularly interesting as virtually all Gaelic Irish surnames include the prefixes 'Mac' or 'O', respectively meaning 'son of' and 'grandson of', which stress the transference of the name from father to son name. This history is complicated, though, because many of these old names were transformed in different ways as Gaelic culture was anglicized as the power of the English crown gradually extended over the island from the late twelfth century onwards.

The researchers applied the MRCA calculation to its surname results and found that, depending on the surname, the date of the common ancestor date ranged widely over the past 2,000 years. Of the surnames with the strongest common ancestor signal, the range of dates for Ryan averaged out at just 650 years ago while for O'Sullivan it averaged out at around 1,200 years ago. (Remember that the MRCA calculation is not exact nor is it a prediction of when the common ancestor actually lived; what it shows is a range of dates within which it is highly likely that the common ancestor lived.)

As I mentioned in the Creer study, another fact that might seem surprising at first glance is that even with those surnames where there is strong evidence that they stem from a single common ancestor, only around 55% of those tested had the DNA signature associated with the shared ancestor. In other words, 45% did not. This may seem a very high figure, but the researchers calculated that the non-paternity rate – 'the historical rate of male introgression' as they described it – required to produce this pattern was actually quite low: only 1 in 60 births would need to be illegitimate.

The researchers found a range of interesting stories about individual surnames. The name McEvoy, for example, was known to have been anglicized from two different roots in different parts of Ireland, a history reflected in the DNA results. Some surnames, such as McCarthy and McGuinness, were found to comprise at least two equally important genetic lineages even though their histories described a single ancestor at their head. In many cases the oral history associated with surnames was gratifyingly confirmed: the McGuiness and McCartan names have a shared lineage history, a story confirmed by the key DNA signature shared by both names.

The researchers also found what they described as 'substantial variance in reproductive legacy' among the single-origin surnames, that is that some of them had created many present-day descendants whilst others now have relatively few. At the top end, the name

O'Sullivan has nearly 40,000 bearers today in Ireland while another single-origin name, O'Gara, has fewer than 1,000.

Mitochondrial DNA

As I've mentioned already in Chapter 5, the nature of the mtDNA test means that mtDNA-based groups are not forming together in the same way that surname-based groups gather together to test their Y-chromosomes. In most cases an mtDNA test, when someone uses it to try to deliver a genealogically useful outcome, is being asked to answer a specific question about their ancestry.

One case cited on the ISOGG website describes a woman who wanted to prove that her five-times great-grandmother along her maternal line was the child and grandchild of two specific women that she'd identified but with whom she'd not been able to show a documented link. After a great deal of time spent on research, a female-line descendant from a daughter of the suspected grandmother was found who agreed to take the mtDNA test. When the two results came back they showed that they shared the same maternal ancestor, thus confirming the connection in the absence of any supporting documentation.

While some people do embark upon their mtDNA test with a specific purpose in mind, many if not most people who take the test do so without knowing what to expect. One story recorded on the ISOGG website quotes the surprise of an American woman named Marie Rundquist who never knew she had any Native American heritage before her mtDNA results showed a maternal DNA signature that is very strongly associated with it. This led her to research her maternal family line back to a marriage in the mid-1600s in the Canadian province of Nova Scotia, where a French settler married an Amerindian woman known only by her forename of Anne-Marie. In this researcher's case, her mtDNA result was a revelation that stimulated her into completing a whole new area of research.

While the ability to find genetic matches within the members of a shared surname is the key attraction of the Y-chromosome test, it is much rarer to find genealogical connections simply by comparing mtDNA results. As you'll remember from Chapter 5, it is very hard indeed to track the maternal line simply because the surname changes each generation. This also ensures that anyone with the same mtDNA result as yours doesn't really know where to start researching to find a connection with you.

Even so, sometimes sheer coincidence will lead a researcher to make a connection because an mtDNA result suggested that one might be found. The ISOGG website cites an example from a project that collects together the results of people belonging to the mitochondrial haplogroup known as U5. The group administrator records that one day she was looking through the family trees submitted by members of the group and was astonished to find the same surname cropping up in two unmatched trees around the same time and in the same location in rural Kentucky. Quite by chance, two people unknown to each other were brought together through the initial link created by their shared mtDNA result, and then the relationship was confirmed by detective work which extended their maternal lines back to a shared ancestor who lived in the mid-1700s.

This kind of luck is still quite rare, and clearly the database of mitochondrial DNA results and linked family trees would have to be very large indeed before this kind of matching process would work on anything other than an occasional basis. But as more and more people take the mtDNA test and the online databases get bigger and bigger, the chances of finding a connection stimulated by a shared DNA result are growing.

*

The stories covered in this chapter are just a snapshot of the kind of research activity now under way among hundreds of DNA research groups around the world. My recommendation to you, if you want to find out more about the successes of the leading Y-chromosome test projects, is simply to visit the website of the most established testing company, Family Tree DNA, and to check their list of projects. These will provide links to web pages associated with each project that will give you plenty of details to chew over. Some interesting ones are collected on the ISOGG website.

Exhumations

There's a time in most surname DNA projects when someone points out that their male line vanished in a flurry of daughters a few hundred years back and asks the question that few dare utter: is it possible to dig up a male ancestor's remains to sample their DNA?

Appealing as the prospect may be to those genealogists who will stop at nothing to overcome a research obstacle, the answer is almost certainly no.

The scientific reason is that genealogical Y-chromosome tests require relatively long pieces of DNA compared to the size of the genetic fragments that generally survive burial in the ground for several centuries. Even if DNA can be recovered from a skeleton, there might not be enough to run an effective test.

The legal reason is that the diocesan authorities are unlikely to permit you to dig in an English churchyard. Back in 2003 historians approached the Consistory Court of the diocese of Chichester asking to open up a tomb in the ancient church of The Holy Trinity in Bosham, West Sussex. They suspected that this is the last resting place of King Harold II, who famously received an arrow in the eye during the Battle of Hastings. The idea was to compare the king's DNA with that of three men — with different DNA signatures — who each claim to be a descendant of the last Saxon king. Not surprisingly, the church court turned down the request.

Chapter 8

How to find or run a project

- Finding a project
- Recruiting participants
- Marketing your project
  Documentation
- Working with your results
  Separating data from information
  Publishing your project report
- A final word

Finding a project

Some of the surname-based DNA projects listed on the websites of the major DNA testing companies have arisen from within long-established family history research groups. If you're thinking of setting up a surname-based DNA project, or even of taking a Y-chromosome test, the first thing you need to check is whether such a research group, which will probably have a lot of information on a number of documented families, already exists. Secondly, you need to check whether a DNA project linked to it has already been launched.

To check the family history research side, visit the website of the Guild of One-Name Studies (GOONS) to see if the surname is registered there. If it is, then you are in luck as the registrant will probably have contact with a great number of family history researchers all over the world and should be able to help you approach potential DNA test candidates. They are also likely to have a great deal of documentary research already collated, which will greatly improve the quality of your DNA project in its early stages.

If your surname is not registered with the GOONS you can double-check whether anyone is collating documentary information on it in a systematic way by posting a message for other researchers on the online surname discussion forums hosted by Rootsweb, Ancestry and GenForum.

To see whether anyone else is already coordinating a DNA project for your surname, first search the websites of the leading DNA testing companies. Those firms that host a significant number of surname projects will have a facility for you to search their database of registered names.

If you find that someone is already organizing a DNA test project for your chosen surname, my advice is not to set up a competing one. If the existing project is limiting itself to a restricted geographical area you may think it a good idea to set up a complementary project covering a different area, but be aware that by splitting the results into two separate projects you will miss one of the key benefits offered by the testing companies: viewing and analyzing all the results for a single surname in one place. A better approach in this case is to contact the existing DNA project organizer and propose splitting the organizational and promotional duties within a single DNA study. One big global study shared between two people is much easier to run, and is likely to be more successful, than two smaller regional studies. This also applies in the case where you'd like to run a DNA project for a surname that could be considered to be a variant of a surname that is already the subject of a DNA project. It will be far more effective in the long run to include your small-scale surname inside a larger DNA project than to run a separate one.

Recruiting participants

One factor in your favour is that the credibility gap that used to exist when one mentioned the phrase 'DNA testing' isn't as strong today, thanks largely to those forensic investigation programmes on television that I mentioned at the beginning of the book. Even so, potential project participants will still find plenty of objections to joining your project, each of which you should be ready to answer.

Email is by far the most efficient and cost-effective way to recruit people to your DNA study. The best way to kick-start this process is to compile an email list of known researchers and surname-bearers. You can then contact them to explain the goals of your DNA project and to provide them with a clear outline of its expected benefits for everyone researching that surname. You may have to build this list of 'sales prospects' up by trawling through the places where researchers congregate online, such as online forums, but you can legitimately pick up names and addresses from public spaces all over the internet.

For each participant in your DNA project you will need to collect details of their genealogy, and specifically details of their oldest ancestor. It is a very good idea to collect this information when they join the project rather than later. You can draft a short questionnaire to send out to each participant that will ensure that you collect the same data from each one. At a minimum this will also include questions about their birthplace, the birthplace of their father and paternal grandfather, and notes on any oral history stories relating to the family. It can also be interesting to ask them about their understanding of the origin of the surname, simply to view the range of different ideas and theories that this process brings forward.

It is a huge task to try to research the family tree of every participant in a DNA project, so be careful not to make that promise lightly! In practice, as the coordinator of the DNA project you're far more likely to let everyone get on with their own documentary research while asking them to keep you informed of any major developments.

If you're without much data on the family trees associated with your surname you will in practice accept anyone into the DNA project with your surname or a variant of it. If you already have some documented family trees to hand you can try to proactively approach living male descendants from the larger family trees. This kind of approach will get your DNA project off to a good start because the larger family trees are more likely to produce the well-defined DNA signatures that you want to use as reference points to link everyone else together.

Eventually, as your project grows, you will want to test more than one man in each large family tree to check that the DNA signature of the first participant is valid throughout the entire tree. When doing this try to choose two men who are related as far back in time as is possible. In any case, do not suggest that two close relations – for example, an uncle and his nephew – take a test. Even if they are aware of the possibility that their DNA results might not match, their test results can add no value to the study as their genealogical relationship is not in doubt.

If the activities described above sound daunting or too time-consuming, you can run a DNA project quite passively by simply registering the surname you are interested in on the test company website and then waiting to see if anyone joins your project. You may be unlucky, particularly if you have a rare surname, and find that no one joins, but in most cases at least one or two people will enquire every year. This kind of passive approach requires a great deal of patience. On the other hand, to accelerate the project you would need to invest time and energy into promoting it.

Marketing your project

Once you've registered your project you'll want to use a range of means to publicize and promote it to existing and potential participants as well as to interested parties in the wider world.

The principal passive method is as suggested above, to simply create a presence on the web to promote your project. The easiest way to do this is to use the space offered on the testing company's website. This will be indexed by the main search engines so that after a few months it will appear high up in the results of any web search citing the surname and the word 'DNA'. Such a web page will be integrated with the testing company's order process, so new participants will be directed to a testing kit order page giving details of the company handling the order, the dispatching of the test kit, and payment.

While you can rely to an extent on passive methods such as word of mouth, in practice if you want your DNA study to grow to a significant size you will need to employ a range of active marketing measures such as those I've summarized on pp. 212–13.

The key to success is to build up an email address list. If you communicate solely by email then the cost to you is only your time. The information you send out need not take long to put together; you don't need to send out a regular email to members of your mailing list more than once every 6–12 months. The progress report on your study could, for example, include a set of statistics on the participants – including, for example, geographical data about them and recording their DNA signatures in a simple table format – with text describing how the study has developed since you last got in contact.

Building up an email list takes time and patience. In genealogical circles it's acceptable to email people you don't know to inform them of your project and the research you are doing, but you should ask them a direct question to get their permission to send them further information at later dates. If they say 'no' then take them off your list! If you're in the UK the present advice is that you are not currently required to register under the Data Protection Act if you are holding this kind of personal data purely for the purposes of genealogical research.

Documentation
As your DNA project gets under way it is a good idea to create standard documentation for all of your participants. This should include background questions about their family tree as already outlined, plus a consent form that gives you permission, as the study organizer, to hold their results, to publish them either separately or as part of family trees, and to upload them onto third-party databases for the purpose of advancing your project.

In the consent form you might also want to include some standard warnings about the undesirability of the DNA testing of siblings, plus a line indemnifying you against any consequences stemming from the participants' DNA results and your interpretation of them.

The documentation you send out to market your project to potential participants should also include a set of reassurances designed to put their minds at rest. First among these is that geneaological DNA test results reveal next to nothing about a person's ethnic origin, appearance, intelligence, medical history or susceptibility to almost any known medical condition. You could add that while some testing companies will hold DNA samples for subsequent reprocessing if requested, every company allows testees to elect to have their sample destroyed after it has been first tested if they so wish.

Working with your results

If your DNA project is registered with any of the leading testing companies, they will inform other clients in their database whenever one of your participants scores a direct or very close match with them. This system of internal matching is a feature that participants can disable if they want, but it is of great value to you as project organizer, as you can use it to connect together members of your own surname project (which is useful) as well as to identify men with other surnames who have the same DNA signature (which generally is not).

When your participants get their results they will want some help to understand their significance and an explanation of how they fit in to the wider surname DNA project. As the study organizer you are responsible for collating, interpreting and presenting the data. At a minimum this means maintaining a list of the DNA signatures together with an indication of which individuals tested in the programme have which signature, plus background information about their origins and their family trees.

It is often difficult to present complex data like DNA results in an easy-to-understand format. Diagrams and tables of numerical data can be worth a thousand words, but try to keep them simple. You want people reading your report to share the emotional excitement of discovery whilst giving them well-documented research data to back up your findings. If in doubt, remember that less can sometimes be more.

What I've outlined in this chapter is, in fact, just the beginning of a surname Y-chromosome study. The real goal of DNA testing is to help people to expand accurately their documented family trees, and in a fully fledged project you will be using the genetic families identified through the DNA results to help them do this.

Separating data from information

The difference between data and information is often not clear at first sight, but thinking about this difference is a good way of clarifying your different roles as project leader.

As the guardian of your project's integrity, your first task is to present the results – the data – in a format that allows easy comparison with the results of other test projects (if you have decided to allow your results to appear online). The second and more demanding task is to interpret them – to take information from them – and to explain their significance both to your project's participants and to a wider audience.

The process of analyzing results to identify matches is not complicated, but there are debates about the number of differences that can be registered while still viewing the own-ers of two samples as members of the same family tree. Each testing company has details about this process on its website to help you.

Bearing in mind that you've already gained permission from participants to include their data in your reports, the two basic sets of result data to be presented are:

• the DNA signatures, i.e. the DNA test results

- the ancestry, lineage and background data relating to each of the DNA project participants.

Keep these separate to start with, and selectively combine them during your analysis to comment on any hypotheses you are reviewing or conclusions you are making based upon the data. Some DNA project websites merge the two sets of data from the start and end up with material displayed with an almost psychedelic intensity, quickly revealing what a tough challenge it is to try to cram multiple layers of data into a single two-dimensional table.

DNA results should be laid out in a table format with the markers set horizontally across the top of the page and test participants listed vertically down the page, as shown in Chapter 2. At every stage be very sure to check and re-check your data. Make sure that you have transcribed everything into your own files accurately so as to avoid any dreaded 'clerical mutations'! Recheck everything regularly.

In some cases it is perfectly possible to handle the process of comparing results on the testing companies' own websites. Some companies have the facility for you to rank individual results in your project and label them as groups. This is a very effective way of sorting results into genetic families, and you can always change the labels at any point. Alternatively, if you transfer your results into your own spreadsheet or database, your options to filter or rank the results is greatly improved. For example, you can arrange to sort your results by the mutation speed of the markers instead of the default order given by the testing company which mixes up slow- and fast-mutating markers. Often the results look a lot clearer if you arrange the markers across the page from the slowest mutating to the fastest. In fact, the preferred order is to start with the haplogroup (either tested or inferred), then secondly to consider the slow-mutating markers, thirdly the fast-mutating markers, and finally the multi-copy markers and the very small group of sometimes unreliable markers.

Publishing your project report
The best approach to online publishing is not to set up a complicated website. It's much more efficient to have a minimum number of web pages to outline the project, and then to deliver the much longer detailed information containing the results and your analysis in the format of a PDF document.

PDF software is very well established nowadays. Downloading the Adobe Reader software and converting your own Word document to a PDF format can both be done for free online.

Your report can also help your marketing efforts. You can email your PDF report to potential project members to solicit them to join as easily as to current members. As your project develops, you'll find it easier to change the Microsoft Word document that underlays your PDF than to update a web page. This method also offers you more organizational flexibility. If you want at some stage to pass on the organization of your surname project to someone else, then someone without web design skills can take it over. What's more, fewer people have security fears when downloading a PDF file compared to, say, a Word document.

The final great advantage of a PDF document is that you can print it out on regular paper from any colour printer without further hassle – so you can conveniently send a copy by regular post to people who do not have email. This is one of the great advantages of the digital age: the ability to create a one-size document that fits all of your different uses.

A final word

You can expect that your project's DNA results will tend to cluster into genetic families quite quickly, though you may also be surprised by how many unmatched results you have. Don't worry about this, particularly if you have a common surname and have relatively few men tested. What often happens is that in the early days of a project the results tend to suggest that the surname has multiple genetic origins. The typical pattern is to find a large number of unlinked DNA signatures. Over time, as more results are collected, the genetic families begin to take shape. As they do you'll feel even more confident in suggesting that your surname has multiple ancestral origins. But as you continue your research, this process often goes into reverse. If you are doing archival research at the same time you may start to find connections between several large family trees that have different DNA signatures, in effect now suggesting that they are a single family tree but containing more than one DNA signature. Suddenly your multiple ancestral origins start to shrink and the surname as a whole begins to look more as though it has a single ancestral origin.

This switch of perspective can be very confusing. The key point to remember is that your project is always a work in progress and that the results circulated are still only a hypothesis. This approach will create time for you to grow your own project and to see how the general process of interpreting DNA results develops over time. Be assured that there are a great many people out there running DNA projects who want to understand the interpretation process as clearly as you do. We're still in the early stages and much more has yet to be discovered about the rules of thumb that will surely be commonplace in a few years' time.

Ideas for marketing your project

- The key to building up any DNA project is to find people who are already interested in their family history to join it. Talk to them and explain the benefits of taking part in your project, or of helping you to find participants. Most genealogists are women, and will be interested in furthering research based on their birth surname, so do enlist their help in finding men to take part in a Y-chromosome project.

- Focus your time by spending it on actions that are most likely to produce results. For example, it's likely that the people you're looking for live in certain parts of the country more than in others:

  - To reach people in a specific locality, call the local newspaper and explain what you're doing; they'll probably love the story you tell them, and the story they publish will give you a great deal of free publicity.

  - Chat to the local librarian and send the library an A4 sheet of paper explaining your project asking them to display it on their notice board.

- Look in the many online phone directories for local numbers, and don't be afraid to call people up to find out which of them already has the family history bug. If people aren't interested you'll soon find out, and there's no better way of identifying those who are ready to hear from you. Many of them will be able to give you details about their tree or tell you who in their family is most interested in the family's history.

- Check whether your surname has a family association. If not, put a notice in the relevant county's family history society magazine asking people to contact you.

- Don't forget to check online to build up a list of email addresses; this is a good activity for a rainy winter's day!

Chapter 9

The future of genetic genealogy

The short-term future of genetic genealogy looks very interesting indeed. The number of people taking DNA tests is growing fast. The number of companies offering DNA tests is also increasing, and the market leaders are offering new facilities to assist project managers to grow their projects. The number of surname-based DNA projects is increasing rapidly, though it is still just a fraction of the total number of surnames in use around the world.

The low-resolution 12-marker tests are now rarely used; they've been replaced by much more powerful high-resolution tests ranging from 37 up to 67 markers. The usefulness of each individual result is growing as testing firms' databases are increasingly made up of high-resolution results. The offer of free, inferred haplogroup results is a huge additional benefit to everyone taking the traditional Y-chromosome test.

DNA project managers have themselves been active in creating new online resources. For example, there are now web pages where you can convert standard Y-chromosome results' data into the various formats required by the specialist charting software favoured by scientists to map DNA results and identify mutational differences.

Other online resources such as databases of results are growing in complexity and usability. Most interestingly, new data about the mutation rates of individual markers is in the pipeline. Some projects which complement their DNA testing with highly developed documentary research activities are in the process of collating their results and may well produce some surprises when they publish them.

In the wider world, DNA testing is moving increasingly into the mainstream. Heritage tests are becoming much more commonplace, popularized by television series such as *The Face of Britain* in 2007 and by massive international projects like the Genographic Project.

There is, however, a lot we are still hoping for.

I expect that in the near future we will see the development of more useful online databases of results. At present the testing firms' databases are light on the kind of background information that surname analysts would find useful to compare the results of different sets of surnames, or to look for regional or clan identities. The next generation of database will probably develop in this direction as the quality of a testing company's results' database becomes the key way in which it can differentiate itself in an increasingly active market.

One offshoot from this will be the publication of data relating to regionally defined DNA signatures, as well as data about the regional distribution of DNA signatures and individual marker values. This will mean that DNA project organizers will one day soon be able to get a closer view, for example, of the results from just Yorkshire-origin surnames and to compare those findings with national averages.

It is possible that the extraction of DNA from household materials belonging to previous generations may become feasible. This could lead to the marketing to genealogists of tests that extract DNA from old artefacts including letters and clothing. One firm is already offering to discuss how it might take a DNA sample of a dead relative from a stamp that they licked. More interestingly, the scope of DNA testing may be expanded through the development of tests that can look beyond the direct paternal and direct maternal lineages to interrogate all of the genetic inputs that make up each of us as individuals.

In the more distant future we can dream of a day when the family history questions that DNA testing can assist us with will be much larger than at present. It may even happen that the entire testing process is dramatically simplified through the development of new testing technologies, which would be a revolution indeed if it led to significantly cheaper DNA testing.

Changes outside the realm of DNA and genetics may also affect the arena in which tests currently take place. The new generation of genealogy websites sets out to generate links between different family trees automatically, an approach to identifying linkages that seems to create a new role for DNA testing to corroborate your findings.

There's never been a better time to be researching one's family history given that the amount of transcribed family history data on the internet is growing very fast. But there is one potential future problem for researchers. In Britain we are witnessing the rapid breakdown of the centuries-old system whereby children automatically take on their father's surname. The process is a gradual one, but genealogists in 100 years' time will surely be warning new researchers that surnames stopped being a reliable way to link families together long before the middle of the twenty-first century. There will be compensations, however: by that time DNA testing will doubtless be well established as an indispensable genealogical tool for building and linking family trees.

Glossary

Terms shown in italics are defined elsewhere in the glossary.

autosomal DNA DNA found in the 22 pairs of human chromosomes, i.e. other than in the sex-determining 23rd pair of chromosomes and the *mitochondrial DNA*. A mother's and father's autosomal DNA is subject to *recombination*, or genetic shuffling, during the process of making the eggs or sperm that will join to create their offspring. Many heritage and *deep ancestry* tests target the autosomal DNA.

Cambridge Reference Sequence (CRS) Reference definition of the *DNA signature* of human *mitochondrial DNA*, first published in 1981 and revised last in 2001.

cell The basic unit of life: 'a miniature factory producing the raw materials, energy and waste removal capabilities necessary to sustain life' (Butler, 2001). The average human has around 100 trillion cells, each of which contains much the same human genetic programming.

chromosome Made of *DNA* and special proteins, chromosomes are the receptacle for *genes* which are arranged along their length in sections known as *coding regions*. Humans have 23 pairs of chromosomes, one of each pair from their mother and one from their father.

clan A grouping of men, based upon allegiance to a laird or chief, and built up through geographical and kinship links. Used to describe kinship groups in both Ireland and Scotland. Some clan lineages have well-defined oral traditions.

clerical mutation A felicitous phrase for human error, it describes any set of false *mutations* caused by the testing lab or project administrator as the result of scribal error. Prone to bedevil even the most carefully organized projects.

coding region Sections of a chromosome that contain *genes* that have a vital or useful function in the replication of a human being.

Data Protection Act Data protection is governed by national law in European countries. In the UK this is covered by the 1998

Data Protection Act which outlines the principles, rules and procedures under which personal identifiable data may be held in the UK. British-based genealogists are currently advised that they are not required to register.

deep ancestry Ancestry prior to the beginning of the standard genealogical timeframe (the period when hereditary surnames came into effect), and stretching back to mankind's origins in Africa.

DNA Deoxyribonucleic acid, the 'read-only memory of the genetic information system' (Passarge, 2001) that resides within each *cell* and which contains the coded instructions required to replicate the cell and associated enzymes.

DNA signature Shorthand phrase to describe the *haplotype* that belongs to an individual DNA study participant or to a group of participants. A DNA signature can exist at different *resolutions*.

DNA test Within a genealogical context, a multiple-marker Y-chromosome test. Can also refer to *mitochondrial DNA* tests and *autosomal DNA* tests.

genes The discrete messages contained in the *chromosomes* that produce all the differences between us. Humans have roughly 30,000–40,000 genes, only several times more than the humble fruit fly.

genetic clan A shorthand phrase to describe members of a *clan* that share a common genetic heritage through identical, or near identical, haplotypes. Popular science writers also use the phrase to describe *haplogroups* and the heads of specific genetic lineages, sometimes giving them fictional identities.

genetic family Shorthand phrase to define men that have an identical, or near identical, *haplotype* or *DNA signature* and who share a common surname. The 'genetic family' is what you create when you aggregate similar Y-chromosome DNA results together.

genetic heritage test DNA tests marketed to family historians that are only rarely of use in genealogy. These tests may use *mitochondrial DNA*, *autosomal DNA* or *Y-chromosome* DNA.

genetics The branch of biology that deals with heredity, the mechanisms of hereditary transmission and the variation of inherited characteristics among related organisms.

haplogroups Large-scale groups of humans identified in studies of ancient human migrations. Defined by differences seen in a specific set of *SNP markers*. Haplogroups are becoming increasingly well defined down in some cases to five or more levels of sub-groups.

haplotype A string of numerical values derived for different markers that collectively make up the result of a Y-chromosome test and define your *DNA signature*. Haplotypes can consist of any number of markers and therefore exist at different marker *resolutions*.

marker The position in the *DNA* where its structure is measured during a *DNA test*.

mitochondrial DNA (mtDNA) The mitochondrion is often described as the *cell's* battery as it performs the essential function of creating, storing and transferring energy within the cell. The genetic code in mitochondrial DNA is passed across the generations from mother to daughter, though every one of us has our mother's mtDNA.

modal A statistical term that describes the most commonly found value among a range of values. In genetic genealogy, applied to the DNA signatures that are the most frequently found among a range of samples.

Most Recent Common Ancestor (MRCA) calculation This attempts to quantify the number of generations since two DNA *haplotypes* diverged from a common ancestor. Potentially this point could lie at any time since the first humans migrated from Africa. The calculation is highly inexact. The results of an MRCA calculation are expressed in terms of a percentage probability (usually 50% or 90%) plus the range of generations in which the result is likely to lie. The calculation is more useful for clan studies which have a longer timeframe than for surname-oriented genealogists who are generally concerned with a relatively short 500-year timeframe.

mtDNA Abbreviation of *mitochondrial DNA*.

mutation *DNA* alters through mutation, which is a slight change in its molecular structure as measured at a particular marker. In terms of the test result the marker value will be slightly different after a mutation than it would have been prior to it, for example 14 instead of 13 or 10 instead of 11. Such a change is described as a single-step mutation, while a change from 12 to 14, for example, would be described as a double-step mutation.

'Out of Africa' thesis Theory, now almost universally accepted, that mankind's origins lie in Africa. Debate still rages, however, about whether the rest of the world was populated by a single migration from Africa or multiple migrations over an extended period of millennia. Built originally around archaeological and palaeo-anthropological findings about extinct human species, the theory was given a huge boost by a ground-breaking paper published in *Nature* by Rebecca Cann in 1987 and subsequently by hundreds of other papers reporting *mtDNA* and *Y-chromosome* results.

recombination An elegant and efficient method for our genes to experiment with gene adaptation without leaving this solely up to chance mutation. The process happens during the formation of eggs or sperm when the two chromosomes in a pair unravel and swap genetic material with each other. From the genealogist's point of view recombination is a problem as it effectively jumbles up any offspring's DNA message. The DNA tests used by genealogists target the *Y-chromosome* which does not recombine during replication.

resolution Every *haplotype* is defined by its degree of resolution. A 4-marker haplotype is not as well defined as a 67-marker haplotype. Genealogists should avoid low-resolution *Y-chromosome* tests and at a minimum chose a medium-resolution test of at least 24 markers.

significance A statistical term and in this context to be used by non-statisticians with care. Genetic genealogists will come across it primarily when reviewing *MRCA calculation* results which are expressed in terms of different confidence levels. However, it also encompasses the art of describing to two project participants whether their results match or not.

SNP markers Abbreviation of single-nucleotide polymorphism markers. At this type of marker mutation occurred only once at a specific position in a particular chromosome in a single individual. SNPs are like an on/off switch that was thrown at a particular moment in time and has not changed since. When you are DNA tested on an SNP marker you will have either result A or result B. The group of descendants that each SNP value defines is known as a *haplogroup*.

STR markers Abbreviation of short tandem repeat markers. The standard *Y-chromosome* tests sold to genealogists all measure STR markers. Test companies like these markers because in the lab they can test for several STRs at a time. Geneticists like them because there are many of them and some are fast-mutating while others are slow to mutate.

Y-chromosome The sex-determining *chromosome* that is present only in males. Mimics the father-to-son transmission of surnames as its DNA is handed down without the shuffling of *recombination*. Surname-based DNA studies should use only Y-chromosome DNA tests for their male participants.

Y-Chromosome Consortium (YCC) Collaborative effort by geneticists to agree a way to describe Y-chromosome *haplogroups*. Its results were defined in a paper published in *Genome Research* in 2002 entitled 'A Nomenclature System for the Tree of Human Y-Chromosomal Binary Haplogroups'. It periodically upgrades its work at <http://ycc.biosci.arizona.edu>.

Useful websites

DNA testing companies

African Ancestry <www.africanancestry.com>

Ancestry by DNA <www.ancestrybydna.com>

DNA Ancestry <http://dna.ancestry.com>

DNA Heritage <http://dnaheritage.com>

DNA Print Genomics <www.dnaprint.com>

DNA Tribes <www.dnatribes.com>

Ethnoancestry <www.ethnoancestry.com>

Family Genetics <www.familygenetics.co.uk>

Family Tree DNA <www.familytreedna.com>

Genebase <www.dnaancestryproject.com>

Genetree <www.genetree.com>

Geogene <www.geogene.com>

Oxford Ancestors <http://oxfordancestors.com>

Relative Genetics <www.relativegenetics.com>

Trace Genetics <www.tracegenetics.com>

Online databases of DNA results

Mitochondrial genome database
  <www.mitomap.org>

SMGF <www.smgf.org/ychromosome/search.jspx>

YBase <www.ybase.org>

Ysearch <www.ysearch.org>

YSTR <www.ystr.org>

Mailing lists

Rootsweb
  <http://lists.rootsweb.com/index/other/DNA>

ISOGG <http://isogg.org/resources.htm>

FTDNA
  <www.familytreedna.com/facts_genes.aspx>

Useful links

Atlas of the Human Journey
  <http://www9.nationalgeographic.com/
  genographic/atlas.html>

Author's DNA website
  <www.DNAandFamilyHistory.com>

DNA links <www.cstl.nist.gov/biotech/strbase/
  weblink.htm> and <www.ethnoancestry.com/
  links.htm>

Guild of One-Name Studies
<www.one-name.org/register.shtml>

The Human Genome Project
<http://genome.wellcome.ac.uk>

International Society of Genetic Genealogists
(ISOGG) <www.isogg.org>

Online Journal of Genetic Genealogy
<http://jgg-online.blogspot.com>

Y-Chromosome Consortium
< http://ycc.biosci.arizona.edu>

Online tools

Convert Word documents to PDF
<www.doc2pdf.net> and
<www.expresspdf.com>

Download PDF reader <www.adobe.com/
products/acrobat/readstep2.html>

MRCA calculator <www.genetealogy.com/
resources/html/cat10.html>

Y-chromosome data conversion
<www.mymcgee.com/tools/yutility.html>

DNA projects mentioned in this book

Y-chromosome

Brazil/Braswell <www.carey-dna.com>

Cooper <www2.arkansas.net/~bcooper2k>

Creer <www.creer.co.uk/index.htm>

Davenport <www.davenportdna.com>

Hurst <www.familytreedna.com/public/hurst>

Kerchner <www.kerchner.com/kerchdna.htm>

Meates <www.meates.accessgenealogy.com>

Mumma <www.mumma.org/DNA.htm>

Pennington <www.penningtonresearch.org/
rc/DNA/dna.htm>

Pomeroy
<www.one-name.org/profiles/pomeroy.html>

Smith (NE states)
<www.smithconnections.com/index.cgi>

Smith (S states) <www.southernsmiths.org/
smithdnaproject.htm>

Steadham <http://homepages.rootsweb.com/
~tstiddem/Pages/dna.html>

Regional

Irish clans
<www.gen.tcd.ie/molpopgen/publications.php>

Scottish clans <www.scottishdna.net>

Shetland <www.davidkfaux.org/ shetlandislands
   Y-DNA.html>

Wales <www.familytreedna.com/public/
   WelshPatronymics>

MtDNA

Marie Rundquist mtDNA
   <www.frenchdna.org/findingannemarie.html>

Genetic heritage

ISOGG chart <www.isogg.org/eochart.htm>

TV series

Blood of the Vikings
   <http://uktv.co.uk/history/ item/aid/528161>

Face of Britain
   <www.channel4.com/history/microsites/H/
   history/e-h/face.html>

Motherland <www.takeawaymedia.com/
   mitochondrialdna.htm>

Who Do You Think You Are? <www.bbc.co.uk/
   history/familyhistory/get_started/>

Further reading

J. Butler, *Forensic DNA Typing* (Academic Press, 2001)

L.L. Cavalli-Sforza, *The Great Human Diasporas* (Perseus, 1995)

L.L. Cavalli-Sforza *et al.*, *The History and Geography of Human Genes* (Princeton University Press, 1995)

L.L. Cavalli-Sforza, *Genes, People and Languages* (Penguin, 2001)

A. Chamberlain & M. Pearson, *Earthly Remains: The History and Science of Preserved Human Bodies* (British Museum Press, 2001)

B. Cunliffe, *The Ancient Celts* (Penguin, 1999)

B. Cunliffe, *Facing the Ocean* (Oxford University Press, 2001)

K. Davies, *Sequence: Inside the Race for the Human Genome* (Weidenfeld & Nicolson, 2001)

J. Haywood (ed.), *The Penguin Historical Atlas of the Vikings* (Penguin, 1995)

M. Jones, *The Molecule Hunt* (Penguin, 2002)

S. Jones, *In the Blood: God, Genes and Destiny* (Doubleday, 1997)

S. Jones, *The Language of Genes* (Flamingo, 2000)

S. Jones, *Y: The Descent of Men* (Little, Brown, 2002)

S. Olson, *Mapping Human History* (Bloomsbury, 2002)

S. Oppenheimer, *Out of Eden* (Constable & Robinson, 2003)

S. Oppenheimer, *The Origins of the British: A Genetic Detective Story* (Constable & Robinson, 2007)

E. Passarge (ed.), *Color Atlas of Genetics* (Georg Thieme Verlag, 2001)

J. Richards, *Blood of the Vikings* (Hodder & Stoughton, 2001)

M. Ridley, *The Red Queen* (Penguin, 1994)

M. Ridley, *Genome: The Autobiography of a Species* (Fourth Estate, 1999)

M. Smolenyak & A. Turner, *Trace your Roots with DNA* (Rodale, 2004)

C. Stringer, *Homo Britannicus* (Penguin, 2007)

B. Sykes, *The Seven Daughters of Eve* (Bantam, 2001)

B. Sykes, *Adam's Curse* (Bantam, 2003)

B. Sykes, *Blood of the Isles* (Bantam, 2006)

S. Wells, *The Journey of Man: A Genetic Odyssey* (Penguin, 2003)

S. Wells, *Deep Ancestry: The Genographic Project* (National Geographic Books, 2007)

Index